MODERNIZATION IN EAST ASIA

MODERNIZATION IN EAST ASIA

Political, Economic, and Social Perspectives

edited by
Richard Harvey Brown and
William T. Liu

Westport, Connecticut
London

Library of Congress Cataloging-in-Publication Data

Modernization in East Asia : political, economic, and social
   perspectives / edited by Richard Harvey Brown and William T. Liu.
      p.   cm.
   Includes index.
   ISBN 0-275-93222-2
   1. East Asia—Economic conditions.   2. East Asia—Politics and
government.   3. East Asia—Social conditions.   I. Brown, Richard
Harvey, 1992.   II. Liu, William T.
HC460.5.M64   1992
330.95—dc20   92-9117

British Library Cataloguing in Publication Data is available.

Library of Congress Catalog Card Number: 92-9117
ISBN: 0-275-93222-2

First published in 1992

Praeger Publishers, 88 Post Road West, Westport, CT 06881
An imprint of Greenwood Publishing Group, Inc.

Printed in the United States of America

The paper used in this book complies with the
Permanent Paper Standard issued by the National
Information Standards Organization (Z39.48-1984).

10 9 8 7 6 5 4 3 2 1

Contents

Preface

In the 1960s, social scientists created "development economics" as a tool for understanding social change in less developed countries, but these new theories largely failed to illuminate the modernization of non-Western countries. Current theories are still inadequate, particularly Eurocentric theories applied to East Asian nations.

The present volume helps to develop alternative theoretical models with particular reference to East Asia. Despite differences in race, language, culture, and institutions—both between and within the countries of East Asia—there are still factors that compel us to consider it as a single region. There is the growing recognition among East Asian leaders that they share many problems, particularly in the area of economic growth. Additional unifying factors include overlapping religious and colonial histories, national rivalries and imperial conquests, similar efforts at political modernization, responses to private enterprise and foreign investment, and regional geopolitics, such as the Sino-Soviet rapprochement. Each of these complex interconnections—historical, religious, cultural, economic, and political—are discussed in chapter one by Richard Harvey Brown, to suggest that events in East Asia cannot be fully understood without a regional perspective.

In chapter two, Gavin Boyd discusses the relations of Japan, East Asia's Newly Industrializing Countries (NICs), and the United States in the world political economy. Today the international political economy suffers from strains in trade and money systems, a slow recovery from recession, and stagnation. Yet, high growth occurs in East Asia, in Japan, in the NICs of South Korea, Taiwan, and Singapore, and in the second-tier NICs of Malaysia, Thailand, the Philippines, and Indonesia. Boyd argues that these nations of East Asia, plus North America, Australia and New Zealand, could achieve export-led growth and redress some negative effects of the international political economy through greater collaboration. However, political and cultural diversities among these peoples and countries may prevent collective action. The high-growth East Asian states are at different levels of development, with Japan being foremost among them. The NICs and Japan limit market access to each other, bypassing potential trade and respective comparative advantages. Similar problems exist between the NICs and the second-tier NICs, and between the second-tier NICs and Japan. Despite such difficulties, however, liberalization of trade in the Pacific appears feasible and likely because of its many advantages.

The success of Japan's economy in the postwar period currently acts as a model for other East Asian nations to emulate in their future economic activity. Government-business relations in Japan are often cited as a key factor in this success. In chapter three, Frances McCall Rosenbluth examines these relations through the case of financial deregulation. It is widely assumed that Japan's economic success has been achieved by governmental policies and leadership, yet the history of government-business relations concerning financial regulation defies this basic characterization. Postwar financial regulation resembled a government-monitored banking cartel that fostered the prosperity of the banks. Although securities firms emerged after World War II, *keiretsu*, bank-centered groupings of firms also emerged, which led to bank-dependent investment and high debt-equity ratios.

In addition, much has been made of the low interest rate policy in Japan. Yet in effect, corporations that depended on the banks for capital paid dearly in interest in the years following World War II. Banks also benefitted through cartel-like *Kisaikai*, or Bond Arrangement Committees, that prevented the development of the corporate bond market. Changes in the international environment now require a switch to banking deregulation in Japan. These shifts in the world economy have fostered a reluctance among Japanese corporations to continue to pay a high price for the borrowing of investment capital. In response, banks have cut their spreads and phased down compensating balances, eased the conditions for domestic corporate bond issuance, gradually lowered the minimum capitalization requirements for issuing firms, and increased the number of firms now permitted to issue debt without collateral. In addition, banks have raised the yields on large deposits, even though this leads to a lowering of their profit margin. In contrast, small deposit deregulation proceeds slowly in Japan due to the absence of an alternative to savings accounts. Thus, argues Rosenbluth, government-business relations in Japan are much more complex and much more responsive to international market forces than previously believed.

In chapter four, Frederic C. Deyo analyzes the interdependencies of development imperatives and social policy formation in East Asia's newly industrializing countries. Social development policy in much of the Third World has been almost wholly driven by political forces. In Latin America, for example, if political opposition severely threatened economic growth, the state reacted by repressing the opposition rather than instituting social policy reforms to accommodate it. In contrast, a less politically mobilized popular sector, as well as a more equitable development strategy, fostered a less combative relationship between the state and the popular sector in East Asia. In addition, the East Asian economic shift from simple labor-intensive export manufacturing to higher value-added manufacturing and services required a social policy that would enhance the skill and productivity of labor. Cross national variation in social policy among the East Asian NICs may be partially explained by differing state activity in fostering economic development, and in the nature of employment systems, which attempt to wed domestic labor to the requirements of export-oriented industrialization.

Over the course of the last twenty-five years, South Korea's economy has been transformed from a poor, agrarian one, to an industrial economy with national income in the upper-middle range. In chapter five, Taewon Kwack reviews this experience and assesses South Korea's future prospects for economic growth. The history of South Korea's economic transformation can be divided into four stages of condensed development: Reconstruction (1950–1961), Export-Oriented Industrialization (1961–1972), Drive Toward Heavy and Chemical Industry (1973–1980), and Liberalization (1980s). Each stage reflects a different strategy for achieving economic development. Several key factors help to explain Korea's economic growth in these stages. Included in these are the role of the government in the strategy of export-led growth, in monetary policy, and in offering financial incentives. Korea's economic structure and its low-wage, highly educated work force also meshed well with the world economic environment.

Economic growth has created tension in Korea, however, because political and social change has not occurred parallel to the economic transformation. The last several years have been ones of both economic stability and political as well as social unrest. Much of the turmoil is attributed to the June 29 Declaration, which promised widespread democratization in Korea, and to the various events that followed. Currently, the most important socioeconomic problem in Korea will likely be providing jobs for the number of expected entrants to the work force. Although Korea will have to meet numerous internal as well as external challenges, evidence suggests that the economy will move toward even steadier economic growth in the future.

The role of the state, labor organizations, and landowners and indus-trialists in shaping national development policies has been the subject of intense debate in advanced industrialized nations, but this inter-connection has received less systematic attention in countries such as Argentina and South Korea. Cross-country comparisons can reveal how the social organization of such nations effects their relative economic success. This certainly is true of Miguel Korzeniewicz and Roberto Korzeniewicz's juxtaposition, in chapter six, of Argentina and South Korea in the postwar era. Indicators show economic decline for Argentina, yet strong economic growth for South Korea. The relationship between labor, capital and the state is a central factor in accounting for these contrasts. Rapid economic growth in postwar South Korea is a consequence of the consolidation of a collaborative interaction between a strong state and an emerging industrial class. In Argentina, in contrast, ongoing sectoral conflict resulted in the instability of institutions and of macroeconomic policies. Timing also was important in shaping the divergent trajectories of Argentina and South Korea. Differences in timing limited and constrained the options available to state policy-makers. In addition, the divergent trajectories of Argentina and South Korea were not discrete and independent events, but an outcome of processes within the world system as a whole.

To explain these differences, the authors trace the evolution of the agrarian class in both Argentina and South Korea. Then they examine differences in industrial development, with a focus on the relation-ship between the state and industrial entrepreneurs. They also explore differences in the structure of the labor force and its impact on labor organizations, as well as the relationship between social conflict and patterns of semi-peripheral development. In comparing Latin American and East Asian countries and their strategies for develop-ment, attention should be focused on the social institutions and social actors responsible for development.

In chapter seven, B. Karin Chai analyzes the situation of Hong Kong on the eve of 1997 as another case of export-oriented indus-trialization and political development. The main vehicle of economic development in Hong Kong has been the policy of industrialization through light manufacturing for export. At the outset of moderniza-tion, the decision-making power of the civil service fused with that of notable entrepreneurs and the traditional elite. The merchants, bankers, and industrialists supported the government and its poli-cies, while in return the government steered clear of policies that might interfere with the functioning of the economy. The alignment of the traditional Hong Kong elite with British colonial powers cre-ated a distance between the elites and the popular classes, resulting in the political exclusion of the popular sector. Appointments to the Legislative Council, Hong Kong's version of a parliament, were primarily based on the appointee's perceived willingness and ability to cooperate with the government. The political colonial system also remained stable due to the continuation of a traditional Chinese political culture that supports autocratic, expert-controlled, and "benevolent" government, and to the widespread political apathy of the population.

Chai analyzes the structure of industry in Hong Kong using organization size as a criterion, in order to probe the situation of the petite bourgeoisie and the working class. The size of organizations reflects qualitative differences in the reproduction of economic classes. Small entrepreneurs, self-employed craftsmen, hawkers, and small shopkeepers comprise the petty bourgeoisie, which appears to be a highly differentiated and transient class, since its members usually expect their children to achieve white collar status. Medium entrepreneurs, in contrast, share the market situation of the bourgeoisie together with self-employed professionals, larger shopkeepers, and merchants.

The character of economic growth and state formation in Thailand are similar to developmental changes in other Third World countries. But as Eliezer B. Ayal points out in chapter eight, several factors are unique to Thailand's transformation to modernity. Of primary importance is the fact that Thailand is the only country in Southeast Asia that was never a colony. Because of this, political modernization and economic development have occurred relatively slowly in Thailand due to limited exposure to Western culture. Other factors explaining a protracted development process include the concentration of the urban population in Bangkok, as well as Thai policies concerning the minority population of Chinese origin. In the early 1960s, Thailand also instituted changes in fiscal and monetary policies, including changes concerning foreign investment.

The period from 1958 to 1973 was crucial to the modernization of Thailand. New external influences on Thailand have led to greater participation in the international community. Inspiration for change has largely derived from the urgings of World Bank missions sent to Thailand, and pressure from the United States for Thailand to be a founding member of SEATO. Other influences include President Nixon's visit to China in 1972, and the unsuccessful United States effort in Vietnam, which reduced United States' credibility as a potential protector of Thailand. Moreover, dependency on the United States has decreased because of the progress of the Thai economy. The economy has largely accelerated due to the export of industrial products, including machinery. Export-oriented activity, in combination with the expansion of the tourist industry and employment abroad by Thai migrant workers, also has aided the overall economy. For the Thai people, exposure to foreign nations has led to new ideas concerning consumption and business, which have, in turn, stimulated an increased pace of economic development.

In East Asian societies, the political class plays a key role in the political life of the nation. The political class supports the state in its interventions and, in return, the policies of the state tend to primarily benefit members of this class. Chapter nine by Albert Celoza is a case study of the role of one political class in the political and economic modernization, or lack of it, of the Philippines. The author gives particular attention to the rise and the demise of the regime of Ferdinand Marcos and the ascent of Corazon Aquino. For Marcos, the strong backing of the political class enabled martial law to become a mechanism for instituting a permanent authoritarian government. Members of this class in the Philippines are the commercial landowning and business people, the managers of bureaucracy (civilian, military, public enterprises, and government corporations), provincial and local elites, and Philippine agents of foreign business interests. This political class makes up a small, interrelated elite. Each subgroup within this elite possesses a singular resource or a combination of resources: machinery and technology, intellectual and ideological skills, control of enterprises or financial capital. This sector of society is also the most highly educated in the Philippines. Higher education further ensures social mobility, as well as influence and access to government services and policy-making. The political class also tends to embrace Western ideas, whereas the majority of the polity remains less affected by and derives fewer benefits from this movement away from traditional values and behavior.

China has historically been the hegemonic power of East Asia because of prestigious civilization, sophisticated military, economic, and governmental apparatus, and its large population, many cities, and huge landmass. Despite its eclipses in the nineteenth century by European and later, Japanese powers, events in China still have major impacts in the Pacific regional economy. This is especially true of the reforms and reactions now being undertaken in China, analyzed by Gavin Boyd in chapter ten. Led by Deng Xiaopeng, China's modernization program sought to build a regulated system of market socialism. Late entry to export-led growth has made it difficult for China to compete with the East Asian NICs for a share of the American, Japanese, and West-European markets. The export performance of Chinese firms has been negatively affected by the persistence of administrative controls established under the command economy, by slow liberalization of prices, and by inadequate development of infrastructure. Inflation, shortages of consumer goods, profiteering, and unemployment also adversely affect the program of economic liberalization.

In the last several years, China's economic problems have worsened due to greater administrative controls over enterprises and markets. Power has shifted to more conservative elite groups in response to the problems of partial liberalization. A further shift of power to the conservatives followed the student demonstrations for democracy in May 1989, resulting in even more administrative control. A fundamental problem for the conservative group now in power is how to promote technocratic modernization while maintaining tight political control. In the Pacific regional economy, China will retain its historically central role only as the policy of liberalization advances.

These essays illuminate the political, economic, and social aspects of modernization. Together they provide new insights and theories for understanding the countries and the region of East Asia, and for assessing the applicability of the "East Asian model" to other areas of the world.

CHAPTER 1

East Asia as a Region for Economic, Political, and Social Analysis

Richard Harvey Brown

The modern "global village" began to appear in the Renaissance of Europe, expanded through commerce and imperialism, and today includes the entire world. No contemporary society is excluded from this global system. We have become interdependent—militarily in our capacity for mutual annihilation, ecologically in our accelerating pollution of the planet, and economically in our global commerce and communications. Unemployment in Youngstown is linked to steel production in Taipei; the price of petroleum in Nagoya is affected by the pride of princes in the Persian Gulf. All such instances bespeak a world system in which events in particular regions and countries are greatly influenced by other, far distant events.

Because of its enormous internal resources and markets, its great political stability, its transnational corporations, and its military might, the United States currently is the major actor on the world stage. Europe and Japan, though political allies of the United States, also are its rivals for the economic dominance of the world system. The Soviet Union acted as a state capitalist in the world economy even before its political fragmentation and economic collapse. As such, it has been part of the global system as a major trading partner and political actor. Today, Russia and its former satellites seek even greater integration into the world economy. China, though a poor nation per capita, is important because of its huge size and population. The same is true, to a lesser degree, of India with respect to South Asia, of Nigeria with respect to Africa, and of Brazil with respect to Latin America.

This global system provides a context in which to examine the experiences and struggles of particular regions and nations in the process of modernization. The masters of modern social thought, such as Karl Marx, Max Weber, or George Simmel, sought to understand this transformation to modernity as it was occurring in the West. In the 1960s, social scientists drew on this intellectual tradition and, in reaction to neoclassical economics, created a "development economics" that focused specifically on the less-developed countries. However, these new theories did not help much in understanding the processes of social change in poorer non-Western nations. Where the theories were applied in practice, the results were disheartening; where they were ignored, as in Japan, economic development was sometimes rapid.

All this suggests that current social theories are inadequate to the complexities of the late twentieth century, particularly Eurocentric theories applied to East Asian nations. Orthodox social scientists retreat into refinements of inapplicable concepts; postmodernists retreat into refined theories of the impossibility of theory; politicians and planners, who have to say *something*, retreat into grand gestures or cynical activism.

An alternative way, which characterizes the essays of this volume, is to accept that our general schemes are outdated and that recommendations derived from them are simplistic. Of course, we may eventually be able to understand the twentieth century retrospectively, with the hindsight of the twenty-first. Meanwhile, we can remain aware of the particular histories of specific peoples, unearth some patterns beneath the irrationality of actions, and thus reveal possibilities that lie in the improbabilities of the modern world itself.

Since the Bandung Conference of 1955, where the term *Third World* was established, the less-developed countries (LDCs) have increasingly voiced their dissatisfaction with the global system and with their role within it. The LDCs have proposed an alternative economic order which, they claim, would redress present inequalities and injustices and thereby alleviate global tensions. But the advent of such a new order is unlikely, because the peoples of the world remain deeply divided in their short-term interests, their institutions, and their symbolic and moral orders. Rich and poor nations thus share their fates within a single global order, but they live in different social and cultural worlds (Aziz 1978).

Moreover, even within East Asia there are enormous differences of history and culture, of politics and economics. As the Indonesian proverb says, *"Lain padang, lain belalang; lain lubuk, lain ikannja* (Other fields, other locusts; other pools, other fish)."* Despite such a recognition by Asians of differences within the region, the concept of "Asia" in the minds of most Westerners has traditionally been taken to mean anything east of the Suez. This is unfortunate in that (setting Turkic, Persian, and Arab peoples apart) "Asia" contains two major historical traditions, those of India and China, which are older and in many ways richer than that of Europe. In addition, a third perspective is demanded for Japan, whose institutional history from earliest times shows remarkable parallels to that of the West. A fourth subregion is constituted by the nations of Southeast Asia, chief characteristics of which are the fusion of Indian, Chinese, and Muslim cultural influences; political Balkanization; and war.

Despite differences of race, language, culture, and institutions, both between and within the countries of East Asia, still other factors compel us to consider East Asia as a single region. The first is the growing concern of East Asian leaders that they share many problems, particularly of economic development. This awareness has been encouraged by their participation in the United Nations Commission for Asia and the Far East (ECAFE), the Asian Development Bank, various U.N. conferences on trade and development, and strategic alliances such as SEATO. Such activities also greatly facilitate intraregional communication. No longer do leaders in Jakarta or Seoul depend, as they once did, on London or Washington for knowledge of each other. Additional unifying factors, discussed more systematically below, include overlapping religious and colonial histories, national rivalries, and imperial conquests; similar efforts at political modernization and responses to private enterprise and foreign investment; and regional geopolitics, such as the emerging Sino-Soviet rapprochement.

OVERLAPPING RELIGIOUS AND COLONIAL HISTORIES

Indians first brought Hinduism and Buddhism to Southeast Asia. They were followed by Confucian and Buddho-Taoist Chinese, who conquered and ruled Vietnam until A.D. 939. Neither Indians nor Chinese made conquests elsewhere in Southeast Asia, but they did spread their ideas and religions. India influenced leaders who used Hindu-Buddhist rites to legitimize their rule. They became the God-kings of the Indonesian empires of Shrivijaya and Majapahit and of the great Khmer Empire, which extended during the ninth to the fifteenth centuries over most of Southeast Asia. Also at this time, Buddhism from Ceylon triumphed over Hinduism almost everywhere. Islam, brought to East Asia by Arab traders, grew in the ashes of the Khmer and Indonesian empires. Later, Christianity was carried by the Spanish and Portuguese to the Philippines and parts of Indonesia.

By the seventeenth century, most of these streams were canalized into the patterns that persist today. Burma, Thailand, Cambodia, and Laos had become Buddhist and were similar to each other culturally and politically. Vietnam had absorbed the culture and institutions of China. Most of the peoples of the Malay Peninsula, Indonesia, and the Southern Philippines had accepted Islam, though Christianity had taken root through Spanish, Portuguese, and Dutch influences. Borneo, Australia, and the Philippines were still largely aboriginal.

In this period, Western colonizers began to make their first encroachments. By the nineteenth century, the Dutch had taken Indonesia from the Portuguese; the British had captured India, Pakistan, Burma, the Malay Peninsula, and Singapore; the Spanish held the Philippines; the French had taken Vietnam, Cambodia, and Laos; and almost everyone claimed rights in China. These powers added a veneer of their respective cultures, particularly among indigenous elites, thereby further increasing the diversity of national and regional identities. As is often the case, Japan was an exception. It remained closed to foreign influence from the seventeenth into the nineteenth century. In about 1630, Japan ended a long period of feudal wars much like those of medieval Europe. During the ensuing period of isolation, Japan created a national government centered in Edo (present-day Tokyo), acquired a stronger sense of racial and cultural unity, and began a quiet commercial revolution.

NATIONAL RIVALRIES

A second factor making East Asia a region is the high incidence of conflict in the area, along with attempts at cooperation. Both cooperation and conflict are forms of interaction, and the increase of both in recent decades has thrust East Asian leaders toward unprecedented contact and interdependence with each other.

It is sometimes suggested that current national rivalries in East Asia merely reflect the spleen of one leader or another who is trying to divert the attention of his people from real problems that confront them at home. On the contrary, many of the conflicts in East Asia are deeply embedded in geographic, economic, and political relationships that have evolved over centuries. Indeed, except for the wars in Korea and Vietnam, the tensions among the nations have not been centrally determined by the global conflict between Communist and non-Communist states, or by the personality of any individual leader.

This is perhaps most clearly illustrated in the border disputes of the region. Not all territorial conflicts between modern East Asian states find a parallel in history, yet even a glance at the ethnographic map of the region reveals continuities with the past. Scores of distinct ethnic groups are surrounded by culturally different peoples.

When conflicts arise, minorities often look across national boundaries for support. Thus, the Shan people of Burma, many of whom want more autonomy or even independence, seek help from adjacent and ethnically similar Thais, and they have not always been disappointed. A similar case is the Muslim, or Moro, population in the Southern Philippines, which has much closer ties with Indonesia than with Manila. The claims of Indonesia on West Iran and parts of Malaysia, and of the Philippines on North Borneo, have similar origins. In cases where the legal border itself is poorly defined, as between Cambodia and Vietnam, the field for conflict is all the more fertile.

Conflicts over territorial rights, though a familiar aspect of international politics, have different roots in East Asia, and Western legal concepts do not adequately describe them. For example, the Khmer kingdom did not wield the kind of political authority or power in all parts of its territory that Westerners associate with the words "empire" or "kingdom." With the exceptions of Japan since the Tokugawas, and China in times of imperial strength, these concepts never implied the territorial sovereignty that developed in the West. The sultans who ruled different parts of what are now Malaya and Indonesia were themselves, at times, beholden to the imperial rule of China, and at no time did they exercise the centrally-controlled and directed rule that Rome wielded over Gaul or the British Isles.

Western legalisms about sovereignty and the state have been superimposed on East Asian traditions. This, plus the parceling up of colonies with little regard to cultural or historical traditions, has encouraged disputes among East Asian nations. Modern Indonesians, for example, often think of their state as the successor to the kingdom of Majapahit. In support of this contention they cite thirteenth-century inscriptions which suggest that the boundaries of that kingdom included much more than present-day Indonesia. Contemporary historians, however, feel that the "empire" of Majapahit may more accurately be interpreted as a series of rulers dominating a sea-based network of island outposts, just beyond which imperial rule ended.

The former imperialism and current economic primacy of Japan also has contributed to a shared identity of the region. The Japanese conquest of Manchuria in 1931, its invasion of China in 1937, its capture of Korea, Taiwan, and the Philippines, and its occupation of Java, Malaysia, and Singapore have given these peoples of East Asia a common, albeit negative, bond. More recently, Japan has been the engine of economic development throughout the region, a source of capital, technology, and markets.

East Asia also has been a region in which a major international political force, Communism, has been functioning for more than seventy years. The careers of Ho Chi Minh and Tan Malaka, the Indonesian revolutionary, reflect this internationalism. Ho, as Comintern and Soviet agent specially responsible for Indochina and nearby areas in the 1920s and 1930s, moved constantly throughout the region. Tan Malaka was equally well-travelled. Marxism asserted that cultural and national differences simply masked the economic plight common to all countries and that their independence required an international victory for Communism. In 1928, the Chinese Communist Party stated that the triumph of Communism in China could not fail to influence neighboring Asia, particularly India, Indochina, Java, and Korea. This is still true of Communist triumphs or defeats today.

EAST ASIA'S MODERNIZING POLITICAL INSTITUTIONS

Traditional societies generally are characterized by paternalistic relations and fatalism, with ordinary people exercising little control over the forces that influence their lives in such areas as taxation, land tenure, or conscription. Poor villagers, therefore, tend to be suspicious and apprehensive in dealing with outsiders. They look upon the government as a distant power and feel themselves helpless as far as significant official action is concerned. In such a situation, it seems absurd to try to change the formal laws. Instead, wisdom lies in seeking preferential treatment in the *application* of the laws, in dealing not with the lawgivers, who are inaccessible, but with the *law-enforcers*, with whom one has face-to-face relations and may be able to sway. One's main action is taken behind the scenes where emphasis is placed not on universalistic conceptions of justice or equality, but on the particular relation between supplicant and chief. Hence, in traditional societies, nepotism, corruption, and pull are of central importance.

In addition to its inaccessibility to poor people, the very weakness of the state breeds disrespect among its own officials. If the state cannot enforce its own laws, corruption seems eminently sensible to civil servants since it involves robbing from the state, which is too feeble to either punish or protect them, and giving to relatives and friends who do have such power of sanction. Thus, the rival authority of the clan or tribe is enhanced to the detriment of a modern state apparatus and a modern economy whose plans and contracts the state must guarantee.

In contrast, modern pluralistic societies have established separate and almost innumerable structures for performing complex and extensive public functions. National energies can be mobilized on a massive basis, but they are not likely to be susceptible to control by one man or clique. Personal attitudes are more optimistic and oriented towards achievement, and relationships tend to be instrumental, universalistic, and rational, in the sense that they are governed by norms such as utility, equality, and legality.

The nations of East Asia, with the exceptions of Australia, New Zealand, and the special case of Japan, fall somewhere between the traditional and modern ideal types. The free press and competitive party system of the Philippines, for example, suggest a modern society, but the dominance by a landed-commercial oligarchy is very traditional. A similar tension between old and new forms exists in Indonesia and Malaysia. The roles of the sultans and old nobility in Malaysia and of kinship ties in the Indonesian bureaucracy are still significant, but Malaysia does possess a competitively entered, efficient civil service, and Indonesia was strongly influenced by the PKI, a disciplined, mass-based political party, until it was destroyed by the military.

These conflicts between ascription and achievement, particularism and universalism, and tradition and modernity can be observed throughout the region. The values of hereditary office and ascriptive recruitment prescribed by a traditional and static society, for example, become nepotism when old values are in conflict with ideas of individual merit and achievement. The value of paying back a personal favor becomes corruption in the context of such modern practices as competitive bidding for contracts or equality before the law.

The states of East Asia thus exhibit features on the same continuum. Most are not so complex as European states where there are numerous veto-holding groups but where centralized coordination is still possible. Yet, neither are they so simple that any one leader can dictate policy, or that no coordination is possible at all. In the Philippines, for example, President Macapagal was not able, despite his preference, to gain necessary popular support for close ties with Indonesia; nor was he able—again despite his wishes—to generate wide support for his claim to North Borneo. Similarly, President Aquino was not able to implement a significant land reform program, despite popular support and her apparent desire for one. On the other hand, until they were overthrown, Sihanouk and Surkarno, respectively, had much greater latitude in expressing their personal will in foreign policy, due mainly to weakness of their nations' modern political institutions.

TRADE AND PRIVATE ENTERPRISE IN EAST ASIAN NATIONS

The countries of East Asia differ widely in their policies governing private investment—ranging from mainland China, where, until recently, all enterprise was state controlled, to Hong Kong, Malaysia, and Singapore, where industrial development has been left almost entirely to the private sector. Other countries in the region maintain positions between these extremes. In Japan, Australia, New Zealand, and Thailand, industrial development has been left to the private sector with a few exceptions, such as the production of railroads and arms and munitions. Public investment, otherwise, only has been in projects for which private capital has been lacking. In Taiwan, Indonesia, South Korea, and the Philippines, governments have played key roles in developing some basic import-substituting industries such as cement, fertilizers, chemicals, rubber tires and tubes, iron, steel, machinery, textiles, and sugar. In these countries, private enterprise also is encouraged, and in Taiwan, South Korea, and the Philippines, the governments transferred some industries to private enterprise after they had been developed. Burma was one of the countries with a mixed pattern until 1963, when government sought to acquire ownership of the entire industrial sector. Indonesia, until the political demise of Sukarno late in 1966, also had a policy of government control over industry, although nationalization generally was confined to foreign-owned firms, and private domestic enterprises were allowed to develop and expand, with the government taking the lead in many fields. Since Sukarno's exit, the new government has encouraged investments from overseas, and many foreign companies have returned to Indonesia.

The international joint ventures most commonly undertaken by East Asians and Western or Japanese capitalists are contracts for managerial and technological assistance, licensing or royalty agreements, loans and deferred payments for the import of machinery, and offshore production or assembly of products requiring low skill and low to moderate technology. In many cases, a combination of these types of cooperation exists. Foreign investment in the form of direct equity participation still is not allowed in Burma, however, but in most other countries, it is welcomed within governmental restrictions on scope and entry. Even Thailand, which, otherwise, has a very liberal investment policy, has reserved several fields for Thai nationals. Others countries have indicated a number of industries in which foreign capital is particularly welcome. In Taiwan, although investment by foreign nationals and overseas Chinese is permitted in a wide range of activities, it has not been allowed in industries whose products already face stiff competition.

The governments of East Asia also can influence private enterprise indirectly through their fiscal and commercial policies. Indeed, numerous laws have been enacted to regulate and stimulate private sector initiatives. In sum, and with exceptions such as Burma and, until recently Vietnam, most East Asian nations have seen government directed capitalism as a viable path to development.

Japan's economic power is another force for integration of East Asia as a region. Relations between Japan and South Korea illustrate this ambiguous role. Many Japanese consider Koreans second-class Asians, as indeed they do all their neighbors. Korea, which was a Japanese colony from 1910 to 1945, remembers the brutality of its former masters. Yet, without Japan, South Korea's dash toward development since 1960 would not have been so spectacular. Japan has supplied the machinery, the know-how, and some of the capital that have helped Korean groups like Hyundai, Lucky-Goldstar, and Samsung to build multibillion-dollar annual sales in the years since the Korean War ended. South Korea is not noticeably grateful. Officials at Japan's Ministry of International Trade and Industry say that large Japanese firms thinking of setting up in South Korea encounter so much bureaucratic obstruction that they prefer to take their direct investment elsewhere. Japan's business role in South Korea remains that of supplier. As a result, South Korea runs a huge trade deficit with Japan. More than one-half of Japan's exports to South Korea are machinery for making the chips, cars, and cameras that are now competing with Japan's own products around the world.

REGIONAL GEOPOLITICS: THE SINO-SOVIET RAPPROCHEMENT

Another factor that brings East Asian nations together as a region is geopolitics. The primary powers of the area—Russia, China, Japan, and the United States—are akin to geological "plates" that move toward or away from each other at almost imperceptible rates until suddenly there are irruptions, such as World War II or the Korean and Vietnam conflicts, which change things dramatically. Three current long-term changes are the efforts of Russia and China to heal the fissures created during the Kruschev-Mao era, the changed status and renegotiated relations between China, Hong Kong, and Taiwan, and the emergence of Japan as a major international political actor. Examination of the first of these geopolitical shifts reveals how the nations of East Asia may be understood as components of a single region.

Since the mid-1980s, both Russia and China sought to reduce foreign tensions and commitments in favor of domestic economic development. China's preconditions for fuller cooperation with Russia were largely met—the rejection by the Soviets of the theory of ideological hegemony and an aggressive military posture toward China, the settlement of Central Asian border disputes, and Soviet and Vietnamese withdrawals respectively from Afghanistan and Kampuchea.

The accommodation reached by China and Russia posed gains and threats for all nations in the region. There were clear advantages for the two principals—more political harmony and less military spending, and greater trade and economic exchange. Moreover, both powers used their growing accord as leverage with Europe, Japan, and the United States.

For East Asia in general, the reduced possibility of armed Sino-Soviet conflict lowered tensions within the region. Vietnamese withdrawal from Kampuchea also helped. Moreover, except for Burma and the Philippines, insurgencies and border disputes were calmer. China became more predictable and less of a regional threat, and the Americans had long been out of Vietnam. There also had been considerable economic development and political liberalization in a number of countries.

On the negative side, however, there was a long-term Soviet military buildup in the region, which continued even as Soviet relations with China relaxed. Against this, the structure of treaty guarantees for Asia included the mutual defense accords that America has with Japan, South Korea, and the Philippines, as well as the SEATO defense treaty. Australia, Malaysia, New Zealand, Singapore, and Britain have a five-nation defense arrangement. When America's tacit defense agreement with Thailand is taken into account, only Indonesia, which may be capable of taking care of itself, remains outside any defense umbrella. The Sino-Russian entente made a shift in regional defense responsibilities from the United States to Japan even more likely.

Of course, various nations of East Asia had their own fears and interests vis-à-vis these regional and geopolitical shifts. For example, the cornerstone of *Japan's* foreign policy remained its relations with the United States, whereas Japan's relations with Russia were kept frigid by the Soviets' continuing occupation of the northern islands of Kunashir, Etorufu, and Shikotan. For Japan, a rapprochement between Russia and China eased tensions in Asia, but it also implied a tacit Chinese acceptance of the Russian occupation of Japanese islands. Japan has been forging remarkably close relations with China. Diplomatic links and commercial relations were resumed in 1972 and 1978, respectively. Japanese trade with China has multiplied rapidly since then. Japanese believed that they could provide most of the banking services China needs, and that they could export ready-made industrial plants that would produce for China's internal markets. Until now, though, Chinese foreign-investment law has discouraged this. For the Chinese, two things about the way the Japanese do business are distressing: their restrictions on technology transfers and, more important, the trade imbalance ($4.2 billion in 1986) in Japan's favor.

Hong Kong's absorption by China, due in 1997, is viewed with mixed feelings there. Thousands of nervous Hong Kongers emigrate every year. Whereas most Hong Kongers are favorable toward the Sino-Soviet rapprochement, many also fear that the energies thereby released in the North may be devoted in the South to reabsorbing Hong Kong. But a majority seems to accept Chinese assurances, written into the agreement with Britain, that the colony's capitalist way of life will be protected under the concept of "one country, two systems." This faith was shaken by the Tienanmen massacre and by China's continuing political repression. Still, China would lose much by interfering with Hong Kong, which is fast becoming a major off-shore platform for investment in, and export from, China, as well as a pole of development in the surrounding Shenzhen economic zone. If Hong Kongers steady their nerves and Communists swallow their pride, the territory could continue to thrive as the gateway to China.

Taiwan also might seem vulnerable to the Sino-Russian rapprochement if China were tempted towards aggression against Taiwan since Soviet military pressure has been removed from the PRC. But this is most unlikely since it would be immensely costly to China's international reputation and its economic and military resources, and might even trigger an American military intervention or a Japanese economic boycott.

North Korea is at a turning point in its relations with Russia and China. North Korea's Kim Il Sung moved toward Russia while trying to keep on reasonably good terms with China, taking full advantage of the Chinese-Soviet relaxation. Russian-North Korean links have been blossoming since President Kim made a visit to Moscow in 1984 after a 23-year lull. The Russians were said to be looking for naval bases in North Korea; their ships already were calling at Wonsan. The Russians also promised help to North Korea's economy under a five-year agreement on trade and cooperation, which will include the construction of nineteen factories. Kim Il Sung also sought to placate his Chinese sponsors and to somewhat loosen North Korea's highly centralized economy.

Thailand was ambivalent about the Sino-Russian rapprochement, but Thailand's security remains guaranteed by the United States and by a withdrawal of Vietnamese from Kampuchea, since this would remove an immediate military threat and permit the eventual resettlement of over 250,000 Cambodians back to their homeland.

Burma's hermit-like nonalignment has depended on Chinese good-will, which continues despite greater Sino-Russian closeness. But

Burma is so preoccupied with its own domestic political problems and with the Shan and Karen insurgencies that it has virtually no policy for the outside world.

Singapore did not greatly fear a Russian-Chinese get-together insofar as Singaporeans, mainly Chinese in origin, believe that, under Deng, China changed sharply for the better.

Malaysia was much more distrustful of China than of Russia, largely because of the support the Chinese gave the country's Communist insurgency in the 1950s. Accordingly, Malaysia has long headed ASEAN's campaign for a zone of "peace, freedom, and neutrality" in the region, which would seek to expel all outside military influence.

Indonesia has the best links with Vietnam and is highly suspicious of China, which supposedly sponsored the rebellion of 1965. Thus, rapprochement between Russia and China was viewed with apprehension by the staunchly anti-Communist President Suharto as freeing both powers for further mischief in Southeast Asia.

The government of the *Philippines* viewed the easing of tension between Russia and China as good for the region and appreciated the lack of strong international Communist support for its own insurgents. There is a Muslim army of 18,000 in the South and a 24,000-strong Communist insurgency that is scattered around the countryside and in the cities. In any case, the external security of the Philippines is guaranteed by the United States, which permits the country to focus on internal political and economic development.

All these complex interconnections—historical, religious, cultural, economic, and political—suggest that East Asia may properly be considered a distinct region, and that happenings in the area cannot be fully comprehended without a regional outlook. Individually and together, the essays in this volume provide such a perspective.

CHAPTER 2

Japan, East Asia's Newly Industrializing Countries, and the United States in the World Political Economy

Gavin Boyd

The international political economy has been affected by strains in trade and money systems, slow recovery from recession in industrialized democracies, and stagnation caused by debt in the Third World. However, high growth has occurred in East Asia. This area comprises Japan; the Newly Industrializing Countries (NICs) of South Korea, Taiwan, and Singapore; and the second-tier NICs of Malaysia, Thailand, the Philippines, and Indonesia. Questions can be asked about this phenomenon of growth. Can Japan, the economic power of the region, aid growth in other parts of the world if its development is largely based on exports? Can other countries adapt East Asian management methods for guiding industrial expansion based on exports? Would Pacific governments with large-scale commerce and links with U.S. transnational companies cooperate economically to promote policies favoring regional trade and direct investment?

East Asian and North American states, with Australia and New Zealand, could collectively achieve export-led growth through intra-industry specialization and trade in a grouping of East Asian and North American states. This would advance market integration if they tried hard to manage their interdependencies. The requirements for collaboration, however, would be very demanding, because firms and countries would gain unevenly. Also, expanding transnational enterprises in the area would tend to diminish the effectiveness of national policies. Because of much cultural and political diversity in the Pacific, difficult questions would, thus, have to be considered about whether such comprehensive collective management would be politically feasible. Interested groups in some of the likely participating countries, moreover, could favor a regional association limited to consultations, leaving each member free to cooperate at its discretion. Businesses in the United States could certainly prefer this since some of their members consider Japan and other East Asian states to have achieved high growth through neomercantilist trade policies that have discriminated against U.S. exports.

The global economy would benefit from the higher levels of growth that could result from regional economic cooperation in the Pacific, even if this collaboration were quite limited because of antipathies, distrust, and unequal bargaining. Commerce with, and direct investment from, the higher growth area would assist recovery from the recession in Western Europe and would stimulate Latin American and African development. In addition, collaboration begun in the Pacific, despite its strains, could help engage with some of the problems of global management, especially to the extent that the United States and Japan could work as partners within the Group of Five and with some consciousness of regional responsibility.

Questions about enhancing growth through regional cooperation are inevitably linked with fundamental issues concerning the ways in which states relate to each other and to international firms. Such questions and issues, moreover, have to be considered with reference to how economic responsibilities of national administration are conceived. In the Pacific setting, the liberal economic thought that influences U.S. perspectives is very different from Japanese notions of guided capitalism. Also, neutral U.S. policies toward transnational production contrast with the external reach of Japan's industrial policy. The political difficulties of working for regional economic cooperation may seem impossible to overcome. The need for such cooperation, however, is becoming stronger, especially because growth problems in the United States have international dimensions, and because the independent activities of transnational companies are continually increasing levels of trade and interdependence of production between the East Asian and North American market-economy states.

EAST ASIAN GROWTH

The East Asian states with high growth are political economies whose characteristics differ at differing levels of development and are linked in a somewhat hierarchical pattern of trade and relations of production. This pattern is changing as the NICs and second-tier

NICs gain comparative advantages while moving to higher techno-logical levels of manufacturing for export. Japan remains central in the pattern because of its large economy and its advances on the frontiers of technology; however, industrial development and diversi-fication in the other states are increasing the scope for intra-industry specialization in relations with Japan. They are also providing oppor-tunities for their domestic firms to move into international opera-tions. Relative bargaining capabilities are thus being altered, although Japan can continue to deal with each state bilaterally, due to little political cooperation between the East Asian NICs and weak cohesion between the second-tier NICs, despite their membership, with Sing-apore, in the Association of Southeast Asian Nations (ASEAN).

Japan's economic policies and the activities of Japanese interna-tional firms are potent factors for integration. The Japanese govern-ment implements industrial and investment policies that seek to locate heavy, chemical, and energy-intensive enterprises in the NICs and second-tier NICSs, together with manufacturing firms producing for the U.S., West European, and local markets. Japanese interna-tional firms, for the most part, cooperate because the culture of their management is strongly national. However, in many cases, the ex-pansion of their vast overseas operations tends to reduce their dependence on support from, and their responsiveness to, guidance by the Ministry of International Trade and Industry. Incentives to directly invest in the NICs and second-tier NICs have increased because of several factors. The yen has moved upward in relation to the U.S. dollar; reserves have accumulated through foreign trade and transnational production; gaining new markets is urgent because of uncertainties affecting commerce with the United States; and in-creased competitiveness is needed to cope with possibly restricted access to the U.S. market and to manage rivalry with the United States in other markets. Japanese direct investment, meanwhile, has become especially attractive for the NICs and the second-tier NICs because protectionist pressures in the U.S. Congress and slackening U.S. growth threaten their revenues from trade with the United States. For the NICs and the second-tier NICs, the most important way of balancing asymmetric interdependence with Japan is to expand eco-nomic ties with the United States. However, levels of U.S. business and official interest tend to be lower, partly because of geographic separation, and partly because imperatives caused by resource defi-ciencies influence the United States' external economic relations much less.

Japan has achieved rapid growth through the official guidance and support of export-oriented private sector development, mainly by informally restraining imports. This has been facilitated by webs of personalized links between firms, and between firms and the national administration. An intense work ethic and strong cultural beliefs in social cooperation, influenced by economic nationalism, have made high productivity possible in Japan. Japanese general trading companies have energetically promoted exports. The U.S. and other Western service enterprises have not equalled this diversified marketing on behalf of small and medium-sized, as well as larger, domestic firms. General trading companies and other Japanese firms, moreover, have undertaken export development and overseas production activities with long-range planning. This has had significant consequences for acquiring market shares and building social foundations for each Japanese presence in a host economy. A willingness to accept minority positions in joint ventures also has been important in Japanese direct investment and has provided a competitive advantage in relation to U.S. firms.

The Japanese strategy of basically self-reliant, export-led, private sector growth under administrative guidance has been followed by South Korea and Taiwan. They have emphasized regulating foreign direct investment and integrating it into industrial policies concerned primarily with enhancing productivity in national firms. Singapore's openness to foreign direct investment has been quite permissive, but at some cost to local firms. However, because of location, this has exposed Japanese enterprises to more active competition from U.S. and West European companies than they appear to have experienced elsewhere in East Asia. South Korea and Taiwan have more forcefully guided export-oriented industrialization than has Japan. When functional, this has aided the prime objectives of penetrating the Japanese and U.S. markets through acquiring comparative advantages that have in part compensated for weak bargaining power on foreign trade issues. Commercial relations with Japan have been basically competitive rather than cooperative, primarily because of the strong social constraints limiting imports into Japan. Larger exports to the United States than those to Japan result in very favorable balances which help to cover substantial deficits in commerce with Japan. This pattern of trade reflects South Korean and Taiwanese dependence on imports of capital goods from Japan and the relatively greater openness of the U.S. market to South Korean and Taiwanese products. Singapore also has large unfavorable balances in trade with Japan, and these, too, are offset, although not so substantially, by favorable balances with the United States.

Hong Kong, a unique entity associated with the NICs, has developed like Singapore, with liberal trade and investment policies, and also has become more dependent on the U.S. market than on Japan's. Large surpluses in commerce with the United States roughly balance substantial deficits in trade with Japan. Hong Kong's trade figures, however, include undetermined volumes of shipments between China and the rest of the world. Transshipments, some from China, also are major factors in Singapore's foreign commerce.

Production interdependencies are associated with the trade interdependencies linking South Korea, Taiwan, Singapore, and Hong Kong with Japan and the United States. Japanese manufacturing in those locations is directed to a large extent at the U.S. market, while U.S. manufacturing in the same locations also is mainly directed at the home market. Conditions in the U.S. economy, then, and changes in its degree of openness, have vital significance for the East Asian NICs and also for Japanese exports of capital goods to the NICs. These conditions also are vital for Japanese exports of manufactured products to the United States, including those sent from Japanese firms and joint ventures in the NICs. Relocating Japanese and U.S. firms away from the NICs would have seriously negative effects on their industrial development. South Korea and Taiwan, however, have significantly limited foreign direct investment, which, at about 5 percent of gross domestic product per year, has been considerably lower than in Singapore and Hong Kong. It has represented only about 20 percent of the gross investment totals that have been facilitating rapid expansion of each state's national firms.

Large-scale relocations of Japanese firms away from the East Asian NICs during a recession in the United States are not expected because these important NICs are nearby and depend on imports of Japanese capital goods. The priorities accorded to them by Japanese investors, however, while remaining higher in the cases of Singapore and Hong Kong, may change relative to those given to the second-tier NICs. This may occur partly because those less-developed, resource-rich states invite manufacturing for their domestic markets and have weaker bargaining capacities in trade and direct investment. U.S. international firms operating in the East Asian NICs would more likely relocate during economic decline in the United States because U.S. management perspectives see East Asia as distant and without high prominence in national policy, ranking next after Latin America as a market for manufactured products.

Economic relations of the NICs with Japan are characterized by limited access to the Japanese market. This, in part, reflects inadequate use both of comparative advantages in low-technology manufacturing and of opportunities to develop intra-industry trade. NIC relations with the second-tier NICs have similar problems. More serious issues, meanwhile, are posed in relations between the second-tier NICs and Japan. Development in the second-tier NICs is lower because of administrative deficiencies, difficulties in completing transitions to export-oriented industrialization, weaker domestic private sectors, and inferior capacities for regulating foreign direct investment. The second-tier NICs compete against the NICs for access to Japanese and U.S. markets, but as exporters of commodities and of modest volumes of manufactured products at lower technological levels. Collective bargaining with the two, large, advanced Pacific trading partners, Japan and the United States, is helped by their shared interests as members of ASEAN. For the present, however, this is of minor importance due to relatively little solidarity in ASEAN and to major differences in industrialization between the second-tier NICs. Indonesia, the largest member of the group, has the most underdeveloped economy and is making the slowest and most difficult transition to export-oriented industrialization. Malaysia, the smallest of the second-tier NICs in ASEAN, is more advanced and has made more progress in manufacturing for foreign markets.

The second-tier East Asian NICs have stronger economic and political links with Japan and the United States than with the NICs. Indonesia's exports to Japan and the United States are proportionally very large—about 50 percent and 22 percent of its total foreign sales—and account for substantial favorable bilateral balances. However, they reflect considerable vulnerability since petroleum exports are high proportions of each total, and the proportions of low-technology manufactures are small and only rising slowly. Malaysia ranks next in dependence on the Japanese market, which receives roughly 25 percent of this country's exports. This dependence is more balanced by sales to the United States (about 12 percent of total) and is moderated by product diversity, reflecting the higher degree of Malaysian industrialization. Thailand, a lower volume exporter relatively more dependent on commodity sales, has stronger links with the U.S. market, which receives about 20 percent of Thai exports. It also has less access to the Japanese market but accepts a relatively high volume of Japanese products, almost 25 percent of total imports. The Philippines, exporting at an even lower volume and even more dependent on commodity earnings, has more substantial economic links with the United States and is less open to imports from Japan. A relatively long period of maladministration under the Marcos regime has hurt that country's performance. Building a new administrative structure under President Aquino and her successors will be difficult and slow.

AN EMERGING PATTERN

The East Asian pattern of economic relations is evolving under strong Japanese influence because administrative guidance in varying degrees controls and directs the outward expansion of the Japanese industrial establishment through broad policies for industry, investment, trade, and finance. Also, the spread of intrafirm and arm's length trade links the NICs and the second-tier NICs with the Japanese economy and its global interdependencies. The extensive Japanese involvement is resulting in substantial benefits for the NICs and the second-tier NICs through technology transfers, the development of linkages with local firms, and large-scale, although uneven, expansion of trade. Major asymmetries in relationships at the official and transnational levels, however, favor Japanese administrative and management preferences, especially because of the pervasive Japanese economic presence. This occurs even where there is caution about accepting increased dependence on Japan, as in the Philippines.

The asymmetries which are sources of influence for Japan derive not only from inequalities in bargaining resources but also from problems of political development in the NICs and the second-tier NICs and from failures in political cooperation between those countries. The South Korean and Taiwan regimes are forms of soft authoritarianism whose technocratic achievements in promoting export-led industrialization are being threatened by populist and distributional pressures generated by the social changes of modernization. Similar pressures on a smaller scale are beginning to challenge the praetorian systems in Thailand and Indonesia. Thailand appears to be moving closer to the Latin American model of a bureaucratic authoritarian regime in the stage of limited pluralism. On the other hand, the Indonesian system remains a form of bourgeois praetorianism with neo-patrimonial features that is not accommodating demands for political participation. Malaysia's basically representative system is under serious communal strain because of the alienating effects of the racially discriminatory economic policies imposed by the Malay political elite. For all the NIC and the second-tier NIC governments under pressure, external inputs into economic growth assume much importance. The prospects of securing such inputs through attracting foreign direct investment for manufacturing and resource development can induce compromises on questions of industrial policy involving the interests of domestic firms.

Indonesia exhibits the most dependence on exports to and direct investment from Japan. This is especially significant because Indonesia needs to raise its level of industrialization for diversified manufacturing aimed at the domestic and foreign markets, as well as to maintain an atmosphere of growth to facilitate social acceptance of continued military rule. South Korea and Taiwan contrast principally with Indonesia because they try to limit dependence on Japan while emphasizing the development of their national firms.

Relative political isolation, however, is a serious problem for both South Korea and Taiwan. Both are very dependent on their links with the United States, a relationship which could be affected by the preferences of any new U.S. administration. Thus, political cooperation between the second-tier NICs could enable them to interact collectively with Japan to manage their interdependencies in ways ensuring adequate scope for expanding and diversifying their national firms. Mutual perceptions of domestic political weaknesses and vulnerabilities, however, discourage understanding and trust between ASEAN governments. Accordingly, Japan can continue to relate to each of these countries bilaterally, with the advantages of greatly superior bargaining power. Furthermore, Japanese firms can relate to governments and local managements with the benefits of extensive informal links extending through their own industry associations to their home administration. Individually, the NICs (excluding Hong Kong) and the second-tier NICs seek to diversify their foreign economic relations, but their options tend to be limited by slack growth in the European Community and stagnation in Latin America. More effective management of their economic ties with the United States is thus becoming urgent.

The challenges confronting South Korea, Taiwan, Singapore, and the second-tier NICs in their foreign economic relations are critical in their efforts to more intensively cultivate domestic political strength, to improve methods of managing the political economy, and to attain greater international competitiveness. Failures in any of these areas can increase risks of internal stress and can indirectly reduce interest in developing more cooperative relations with other NICs and second-tier NICs in East Asia. None of the leaderships in these states have distinctive capabilities for such political entrepreneurship. Moreover, attempts at such cooperative linkages would be hindered by the ethnic, cultural, and political differences between these East Asian states, as well as by divergences in official perceptions of external economic interests. The second-tier NIC governments have tended to see their countries competing against each other in sales of commodities and low-technology manufactures to advanced country markets, in the development of new industrial capacities, and in attracting foreign direct investment. Attempts at industrial cooperation for complementary development within ASEAN have been rather unsuccessful. The limited functions assigned to the ASEAN Secretariat, moreover, have tended to prevent it from assuming planning and advocacy roles that could encourage productive interactions between the member states.

Altogether, the main characteristics of the East Asian economic relations and its evolution allow extensive scope for Japan to consolidate its strong central position. Increased outflows of Japanese direct investment are tending to link the NICs and second-tier NICs more closely with the Japanese economy, as has been stressed. On the other hand, the advantages of Japanese international firms, caused by the scale of their activities and their technological advances, are increasing relative to the capabilities of firms based in the NICs and second-tier NICs. The Japanese enterprises are tending to gain technologically-based oligopoly power in East Asian markets, while smaller firms in the modernizing, East Asian, market-economy states experience reduced competitiveness and have to cope with more barriers to entry. On the Japanese side, the drive for regional and global market penetration remains strong and may even be increasing because of the new problems that have been noted concerning economic trends in the United States and changes in U.S. trade policy.

Change in the Japanese political economy, however, can affect its role in the region. Large-scale shifts to overseas production, as the current outflow of direct investment continues, tend to reduce investment in domestic plants. Such investments at home also are tending to decrease because of more attractive foreign portfolio investment with the upward movement of the yen. Productivity in domestic production facilities may thus decline, even as unemployment increases due to losses by subcontracting companies in Japan. Employment in the service industries will increase, but manufacturing employment will decline. The efforts of Japanese managements to achieve rapid technological advances through home-based research and development will work against any trend toward decline in domestic productivity. This will continue to be a high priority and to direct overseas production activities for global market penetration. Thus, highly specialized production activities for global market penetration will be retained in home country plants.

Change in the NICs and second-tier NICs may well follow economic strains in Japan, especially because those developing states are not as adaptable as the Japanese political economy and have less significant options for diversification of external trade. Pressures for more equitable internal distribution and demands for wider political participation in the NICs can be expected to increase, whereas trade-induced growth will slacken with slower increases in exports to Japan and the United States. The legitimacy problems of some of the more authoritarian NICs and second-tier NICs may thus become serious. The modest processes of cooperation within the ASEAN would then be weakened as domestic concerns of member government became more intense. Mutual perceptions of political vulnerabilities would reduce interest in collaborating and induce more local protectionism. Of course, continued economic growth in the NICs and second-tier NICs may gradually ease problems of political development. However, present indications are that this is not likely to inspire any major Japanese initiatives for East Asian partnership in development, even though that would accord with long-term Japanese, NIC, and second-tier NIC interests.

EAST ASIA AND THE PACIFIC

The relations between East Asian states with market economies, though generally substantial and increasing, are, nevertheless, smaller overall than their interdependencies with the United States. The bonds with the United States are extensive and complex, comprising mainly Japan's high volume commerce and cross investment, but also including NIC and second-tier NIC trade and production ties with the United States. These are ties in which Japanese and U.S. firms play important roles. Japan sends roughly one-third of its exports to the United States—slightly more than all of its exports to the Third World, about 50 percent more than its exports to the rest of Asia, and about three times its exports to the European Community. The exports to the United States, moreover, are increasing much faster than those to the European Community and to the rest of Asia. Japanese direct investment in the United States, which totaled roughly $10 billion in 1982, is about 35 percent of the country's total foreign direct investment. At its present rate of expansion, it will have increased ten times above the early 1980s level by the year 2000. A substantial volume of the direct investment flowing into other Asian countries, which is altogether roughly half the flow into the United States, appears to be related to manufacturing aimed at the U.S. market. For the United States, trade links with Japan, the NICs, and the second-tier NICs are becoming as extensive as those with the European Community and are growing faster, although with considerable imbalances. Production by U.S. firms in the European Community is much larger than U.S. production in East Asia. However, the future of European-based production and of exports to the European Community is less favorable than the outlook for U.S. commerce with and direct investment in East Asia because of slower growth in the West European economies.

The trade and production links between East Asia and the United States are evolving in a policy environment shaped almost entirely by Japanese and U.S. administrations. The level of policy interdependence is high, especially because of the broad scope of measures adopted on the Japanese side, and also because of Japanese sensitivity to any leverage exerted by the U.S. administration. The United States mainly initiates interactions because of dissatisfaction with

its large bilateral trade imbalance, but these tend to be rather unproductive. Mixes of noncooperative and cooperative behavior at
the governmental level allow relations at the level of transnational
firms to continue. At this level, Japanese firms enjoy advantages in
production and marketing that result from their home administration's support, as well as from their mutual ties and the overall level
of efficiency of their political economy. The Japanese policy style is
holistically rational, anticipatory, and broadly consensual, largely
due to guidance by an enterprising bureaucratic elite. Fiscal, monetary, financial, industrial, investment, and trade measures are integrated in a wide-ranging neomercantilist design that includes elements
of a strategic commercial policy. Japanese international firms, to a
large extent, collaborate with this design on the basis of strong home
country ties, and their overseas operations, to a degree, extend economic sovereignty. U.S.-based international firms have much weaker
home country ties, tend to lose these rapidly, and operate with exclusive concerns for their own interests that entail losses of U.S. economic
sovereignty. The U.S. administration distantly manages relations with
American international firms. The various areas of U.S. economic
policy tend to be uncoordinated and shaped by highly pluralistic
policy processes in numerous centers of power whose effectiveness
tends to be determined more by influence than by jurisdiction. The
overall policy style is cybernetic, reactive, conflicted, and vulnerable
to shifts in idiosyncratic preferences of changing executives.

The U.S. policy orientation is basically liberal, although possessing
some tacit neomercantilist elements, and reflects strong culturally-
based confidence in the effectiveness of market forces and in market
justice. It also reflects a distrust of power, an important feature of
the American political culture, and a fear that developing close government-business relations would generate much corruption and
inefficiency. Pressures of political competition in the U.S. system,
however, have been causing U.S. administrations to become increasingly involved in the economy, domestically and externally. Such
involvement tended to increase in response to foreign trade and investment issues that affect politically important domestic interests.
Moreover, in recent years, public debate has weakened the beliefs of
political and business leaders regarding the efficiency and welfare
results of free market forces. This debate has increased general
awareness that the governments of major trading partners have fixed
interventionist orientations, that foreign firms have acquired competitive advantages from forms of government aid over long periods,
and that the experience of interventionist government has demonstrated the potential benefits of industrial policies. Moreover, the
globalizing of operations by footloose firms that are acquiring oligop-

oly power in the world markets is raising new questions about market forces because such firms expand by internalizing markets.

Although the U.S. policy orientation remains fundamentally liberal, it is being influenced by strong competitive concerns and by strongly felt imperatives to retaliate against governments believed to be guilty of unfair trade practices and of restraining internal demand. Consciousness of strong national bargaining power, however, is responsible for inclinations to resort to leverage against governments considered uncooperative. There can be political benefits for an administration that engages in public leverage if this secures accommodation from a foreign state and is thus viewed favorably by U.S. legislators and the U.S. media.

Economic policy interactions between Japan and the United States reveal failures of negotiation and cooperation. These can be attributed to diverging policy styles and orientations and to the large imbalances at the transnational level in benefits derived from commerce and transnational production. Differences in bargaining capacity and commitment have affected the significance of these long-standing features of the relationship in complex ways. In recent years, the vulnerabilities of policy interdependence and transnational interdependence have become more constraining for each side because of the substantial flow of Japanese loan funds into the United States. These funds have supported government borrowing to cover the U.S. budget deficit and the growing volume of Japanese direct investment in the United States. These widely understood restraints on noncooperative behavior have increased the urgency to collaborate in managing the intricate interpenetration of the two political economies. The interests of the East Asian NICs and the second-tier NICs, as well as of Canada, Australia, and New Zealand, are vitally affected by trends in the U.S.-Japan relationship. However, no regional organization exists through which they can participate in the settlement of issues affecting that relationship. Also, they have little significant involvement in the global economic organizations, OECD and the IMF, that are concerned with U.S.-Japan frictions in international trading and monetary systems.

The principal trends in U.S.-Japan economic policy interactions concern functional imperatives for cooperation, shifts in policy styles and orientations, and the continuing expansion of transnational links. On the Japanese side, there is a high degree of continuity in policy and implementation. This can be attributed to the breadth of policy consensus in the political and economic elite, to the very substantial gains from neomercantilism, to the acute awareness of resource deficiencies, and to perception of isolation in an unfriendly world. The introduction of elements of economic liberalism into Japan's established policy orientation is largely precluded by recognition of the efficiency of the national system of guided capitalism and that it must be maintained to maintain and increase global market shares. The United States' current difficulties in macromanagement are seen as indicating the defects of liberal economic thought and the consequences of lower levels of overall efficiency in a pluralist state. There is evidently a tacit understanding, moreover, that a firm basis for comprehensive cooperation with the United States would be difficult to negotiate because of the strong pluralism in the U.S. system and, even if achieved, would be subject to unilateral adjustment by the U.S. side because of shifts in the preferences of successive presidents. The rational method of managing the relationship, then, is evidently seen to be short-term adjustment through incremental accommodation. That means responding to U.S. demands for expansionary measures and market access while adding to the gains from commerce and overseas manufacturing and ensuring that these contribute to advances on the frontiers of technology for further productivity.

In the United States, large bilateral imbalances have provoked intense activity within the extensive trade policy community. At the same time, issues relating to the international role of the dollar have continued to be very much confined to the Treasury and the Federal Reserve system. Although fiscal policy has become a matter of reluctant bipartisan engagement, decisions are discouraged by the political costs of remedies for budget deficits. Monetary policy is the most significant area of executive choice because of congressional roles in trade and fiscal policy. Although the options are difficult, there is a trend toward a looser approach that will further lower the value of the dollar, thus tending to reduce Japan's export earnings but facilitating Japanese direct investment in the United States. In trade policy, there are strong political incentives to move toward wider, sectorally managed foreign commerce. This would limit the disruption of internal markets through surges of imports, reduce vulnerability to foreign strategic trade policies, and gain support from alienated interest groups and legislators. Such a choice has become attractive because of the strength of Democrats in Congress and because of a general decline of confidence in GATT agreements as restraints on foreign government use of nontariff barriers and subsidies. If trading partners accepted sectorally managed commerce, moreover, the United States could utilize its superior bargaining power to impose its preferences. It could make swift adjustments while setting precedents for departures from GATT principles that emphasize its capacity for leverage. Reducing the trade deficit through managed commerce would also reduce the need for currency depreciation as an aid to trade policy. Of course, inflows of Japanese direct investment would be further encouraged, but with less serious competitive implications for U.S. firms. It must be stressed, however, that Japan's accumulation of favorable trade balances is evidently tending to enhance political incentives to opt for managed trade on a fairly extensive scale.

The major challenge that must be anticipated by Japan, therefore, is selective reduction of access to the U.S. market. This would have the likely benefit of reduced upward pressure on the yen, aided by some improvement in the U.S. trade balance and continued large-scale borrowing by the U.S. administration. The responses of the large Japanese policy communities will probably await clear identification of the trend in U.S. policies; however, while in the period of uncertainty now beginning, there will, no doubt, be emphasis on facilitating direct and portfolio investment in the United States and developing joint ventures between major Japanese and U.S. firms. Moderately expansionary measures may well be adopted but primarily to aid the political fortunes of the liberal Democratic Party rather than to increase consumer demand for U.S. products. Administrative nontariff barriers may be reduced, but there will be no question of attempting to change the vast pattern of administrative guidance and relational, rather than arm's length, contracting which sustains the overall level of efficiency.

The problems of bilateral management between the United States and Japan overshadow the regional concerns of the smaller Pacific states, and among these is the Association of Southeast Asian Nations, the only group which could represent collective interests. This association distantly and intermittently interacts with the United States, Japan, South Korea, Canada, Australia, and New Zealand, maintaining consultative links in which information and views are exchanged on questions of liberalizing regional trade and investment. Private groups in most of these countries advocating regional economic cooperation have received significant official encouragement, especially in Japan. Through occasional dialogues, ASEAN members and other Pacific states have been able to introduce suggestions for forming a Pacific Community. Most of the ASEAN governments, however, are apprehensive that the United States and Japan would dominate the proposed regional organization and do not envisage building political links with Canada, Australia, New Zealand, and South Korea that would, to some degree, offset U.S. and Japanese influence. Hence, the United States and Japan relate to each other without the informal accountability to other Pacific states that would develop in an emerging regional economic community.

ISSUES OF REGIONAL COOPERATION

The magnitude of political and economic issues between the United States and Japan has tended to obscure imperatives for multilateral cooperations that are posed in the regional setting of high and rising interdependencies. Such cooperation would enhance trade and encourage specialization of production on a wider scale. Cooperation also would foster collective export-led growth, with expanding intra-industry commerce at ascending technological levels. Such needs and imperatives for such cooperation can be conceptualized not only in terms of the regional common interest, but also with reference to North–South as well as North–North issues.

Regional cooperation can be envisaged simply in terms of laissez-faire trade liberalization, with expectations of increased efficiency and welfare, and possibly of policy learning, in line with neofunctional logic, that will lead to the coordination of fiscal, monetary, and investment, as well as trade, policies. The cultural and political diversity of the East Asian and Pacific market-economy states has tended to convince many advocates of Pacific regional cooperation that only a loose consultative association oriented towards laissez-faire trade liberalization will be politically feasible. This view has tended to gain acceptance in part because of the influence of pragmatism in U.S. and in some East Asian policy communities—pragmatism that distrusts analysis and planning, and that results in tending to wait upon events, as well as adopting experimental and incremental approaches to policy issues, with ambivalence between considerations of functional and political exchange.

The case for working toward more than laissez-faire trade liberalization in the Pacific setting, despite its diversity, can emphasize the creation of a framework of concerted policies. In this framework, the strained relationships between the two largest economic powers can be transformed into a partnership, despite their opposed policy orientations, which can constitute an appropriate environment for the development of China's emerging international economic interdependence. Laissez-faire trade liberalization in the region would enhance growth through specialization and economies of scale. However, the spread of benefits between countries and firms would be uneven because of differences in levels of development and capacities and preferences for the use of neomercantilist measures within limits that less advantaged states in the grouping would be induced to tolerate, given expected inequalities in bargaining power. Depending on the terms and phases of the liberalization process, Japan would benefit more than the United States, and both would benefit more than the NICs, the second-tier NICs, and the small industrialized Pacific states. The dissatisfaction of these states would strain the arrangements for less restricted commerce, but Japanese and U.S. responses to this probably would not be sufficiently accommodating. Policy communities in both states would tend to be excessively confident in their national bargaining strengths and would tend to be influenced by the representations of firms extracting substantial profits from operations in the relatively integrated regional market. Meanwhile, unless ways were found to stabilize the U.S. dollar, exchange rate volatility would affect the usefulness of market integration. This volatility would tend to dampen growth and somewhat discourage trade, with increasing incentives to produce in foreign markets rather than to export to them. Japanese firms could cope more easily with such an operational environment than their counterparts based in other Pacific countries and the United States. A strong reason for monetary cooperation can thus be seen if benefits of growth from a liberalization of regional trade are to be sought.

To advance beyond the inevitably unstable elementary level of regional integration, however, would require key members to address and resolve key issues concerning the structuring of collective decision-making for regional cooperation. Questions about the political feasibility of alternative solutions could be very difficult. Because of the breadth of the policy collaboration needed for a viable regional community, governments could be very unwilling to sacrifice any degree of independence by participating in confederate decision processes. They could be even more unwilling to entrust significant powers to a common institution that might be set up through confederate or majority choice.

Yet, elite attitude toward, and estimates of, the political feasibility of options for regional cooperation could change. This could happen through experiences of productive collaboration. Such experiences could be made possible through various methods promising high utility with low risks. One possibility would be the convening of direct investment planning conferences, for example, under U.S., Japanese, and ASEAN auspices. ASEAN participation could be reluctant, of course, because of apprehension about U.S.-Japanese collaboration to exploit the weak bargaining power of the second-tier NICs. Such fears, however, could be moderated if ASEAN became a more cohesive and institutionally more advanced organization.

For the governments of market-economy East Asian and Pacific states engaged in regional cooperation, the prime considerations would concern relationships between perceived national interests and prospective collective benefits. Questions about China's role in the Pacific would tend to be regarded as peripheral because of uncertainties about the evolution of Chinese policies and general awareness of a persistent emphasis on independence and self-reliance in China's external relations. Developing an efficient and equitable system of Pacific regional cooperation, however, would tend to strengthen the commitment of Chinese elites to constructing a form of market socialism with a growing sector of guided capitalism. Higher growth in the Pacific, moreover, would hold out prospects for higher trade-induced growth in China and also aid the evolution of less totalitarian Chinese political philosophy and practice that allowed the freedoms necessary for greater systems efficiency.

THE PACIFIC AND THE GLOBAL ECONOMY

For states outside the Pacific, and for the United States and Japan as members of the Group of Five, the possibilities for attaining higher growth in East Asia and North America through regional cooperation have special significance. Enhanced commerce and more active transnational relations with a Pacific economic community would assist recovery from the recession in the European Community and help rehabilitate the debt-burdened economies of Latin America, Africa, and South Asia.

For the global economy, the most important relationship would be that with the European Community. Either this could evolve distantly, considering European disinterest in the problems of the Pacific and a readiness to await initiatives from Pacific states, or Europe could constructively engage in the political economy issues of the Pacific. This could assist in developing an elite consensus in that area on principles of regional cooperation, through conferences drawing on the European Community's own experience. A transregional partnership for growth would be possible rather than the competitive and, in some ways, adversarial interaction envisaged if a Pacific organization for economic cooperation brings the United States and Japan closer on the basis of shared ambitions for global market power and to the exclusion of the European Community's firms from the NICs and second-tier NICs. With a European-Pacific partnership, moreover, the difficult tasks of global management would be made easier. Two large patterns of regional cooperation would be brought into harmony with a broad aggregation of interests, providing a basis for collectively directing international trade and monetary regimes. The present system of U.S. domination of the Group of Five through bilateral interactions with West Germany and Japan, and exclusive Group of Five caucusing within OECD, the IMF, and the World Bank would be replaced through restructuring that would give those global organizations a more representative quality. At that level, more substantial functions for global management could be assumed, that is, with institutional development expanding collective responsibilities while reducing the dependence of international cooperation on the preferences of the U.S. administration. This change would result in increased international accountability for all members of the Group of Five and thus, might help them to resolve certain problems of governance because of intensified international policy-learning by their elites.

The requirements for regional and transregional cooperation tend to be overlooked in much international political economy literature, mainly because of interest in the potential gains from advances toward global market integration. This interest has been aroused because of the weakening of the GATT system and the spread of managed trade, protectionist measures, country trading, and strategic trade policies, as well as the use of fiscal, monetary, and investment measures to influence terms of trade and trade flows. The concerns with trade, however, have considerably hindered recognition of the degree to which trade is being dominated by international firms. Such firms are internalizing markets and acquiring oligopoly power that is making markets less contestable, while substituting transnational production for arm's length trade. Also escaping notice is the degree to which international firms are evading national jurisdictions and basing their cooperation with such jurisdictions on toleration of their overall endeavors to strengthen their independence from most forms of state control.

The main implication of the growth of global market power by mostly footloose international firms is that the relative openness of national economies makes them vulnerable to disruptive surges of imports and to shifts of production processes from one nation to another. To secure adequate growth-inducing benefits from liberalized trade, therefore, integrated markets must be made contestable with investment and industrial measures to regulate international firms. This must be undertaken at the regional level if it is to be reasonably effective and equitable. At the global level, it would be unmanageable, while at the national level, the efforts of governments to protect their economies against disruptive imports would tend, as at present, to limit gains from trade. Regional economic cooperation can thus be seen as combining the advantages of market integration with the benefits of collective regulative activity that can reduce market failure. Further reduction of such elements, moreover, could be feasible at the regional level, as has been suggested, through new service enterprises.

With this perspective, the rationale for Pacific economic cooperation becomes more persuasive, subject to considerations of political feasibility. At the same time, the importance of transregional cooperation also becomes clearer. Transregional cooperation can bridge the gap between regional and global levels. Regional systems of collective management, by concerting the trade, industrial, investment, fiscal, and monetary policies of members states, would develop collaboration with other regional systems. Appropriate orientations for using those capabilities could be anticipated in the European-Pacific context if initiatives were taken on each side to build the necessary consensus in elite networks. Such initiatives may not be expected on the European side in view of the problems of completing market integration within the European Community, but certainly the Community is being challenged to expand its commerce with the high-growth East Asian area. This challenge can be met most effectively by combining constructive political engagement with extended trade and investment. Also, the Community is being challenged to cope with problems of global management made difficult by failures of macromanagement in the United States, which may lead to a worldwide recession. To work effectively toward solutions for these problems, the European Community will certainly need the cooperation of Japan and will be assisted even more if support from a group of Pacific states becomes possible.

PROSPECTS

The suggestions for collective management at the Pacific and Euro-Pacific levels indicate a need for political entrepreneurship. Although forms of cooperation can be proposed with neofunctional expectations of policy-learning and interest group support, advances toward institutionalized collaboration are not likely without intensive diffuse leadership. This will have to be aimed at promoting broad elite consensus on a doctrine of concerted macromanagement, intergovernmental bonds on a large scale, regionalization of interest groups, and common institutions for advocacy and decision-making. Such institutions would be based on aggregations of regional concerns and on independent planning capabilities.

Initiatives on the Pacific side could be encouraged within ASEAN and within the private regionally-oriented Japanese and American groups advocating the formation of a Pacific Community. Japanese government initiatives would respond to U.S. and other exhortations about the need for more active Japanese leadership in world affairs, but in addition to requiring domestic consensus, such initiatives would have to be encouraged by some inviting new trends in regional politics. Endeavors by the U.S. administration to promote Pacific and Euro-Asian cooperation are not to be expected for the present because of preoccupation with the budget and trade deficits and with stock market and exchange rate volatility. However, all those problems would be made more manageable through a Pacific economic community linked through wide-ranging cooperation with Western Europe.

The prospect of inaction on the Pacific side makes it necessary to consider what might be undertaken by European groups and by the European Community. West European disillusionment with U.S. leadership in the international political economy has been increased by stock market falls and the United States' unilateral moves towards currency depreciation. The principal challenge for the European Community, however, is to assert a strong new role in world affairs with which the United States will have incentives to cooperate and to develop a more constructive U.S. global role through mutual ac-countability. If this is to happen, it will have to be promoted by the Franco-German coalition which virtually dominates European Com-munity decision-making. Extensive conferencing under the auspices of European public policy institutes would have to generate the wide support needed within the Community.

The rationale for engagement in the Pacific and for promoting transregional cooperation may well become more persuasive for European Community elites because of growing awareness of tech-nology-driven factors that are tending to make the oligopoly power of U.S. and Japanese firms a more serious problem in world markets. While competitive pressures tend to push up technological levels in most areas of manufacturing, firms whose competitiveness depends increasingly on using advances in frontier technology have active in-terests in collaborating with other enterprises operating at the same level and already having extensive market shares. Such cooperation is necessary to gain access to new technology as well as for collabo-rative market domination. Incentives for firms to cooperate with national industrial strategies generally become weaker than the in-centives for oligopolistic technological cooperation. This has signifi-cant implications for West European enterprises and administrations. This judgment has to be qualified in cases of Japanese firms because of their strong national ties. Even so, this must be done in a way that adds to the significance of the general observation regarding the interests of West European companies.

What can be suggested for European involvement in the Pacific, then, must be seen with reference not only to transregional benefits but also to the global problems of collective management. The in-creased needs for order and growth with equity in the world economy will have to be met with widening application of the lessons of the European experience at the regional level. If this can be done in the Pacific, some major advances in restructuring presently inadequate global economic institutions will be possible.

CHAPTER 3

Government-Business Relations in Japan: The Case of Financial Deregulation

Frances McCall Rosenbluth

Japan's pattern of economic success is often raised as a model for the rest of East Asia. Before citing the shared Confucian legacy, similar geopolitical attributes, or the role of the "strong state," however, we need a clearer picture of what the "Japanese model" actually is. The history of government-business interaction in Japan's financial regulation casts serious doubt on the common characterization of Japan's economic performance as government-led. Rather than utilizing the financial system as an instrument of state policy, the Japanese government has in large part responded to the interests of the well-organized and politically influential banks in formulating financial regulation. Early postwar financial regulation was akin to a government-monitored banking cartel. Now deregulation is proceeding because changes in the international environment have rendered the original protective regulation no longer advantageous to the banks that benefited from the rules in the first place.

The Ministry of Finance (MOF) is the primary government actor involved in financial regulation, and it takes considerable pains to obviate the direct interference of politicians or other outsiders. To thereby conclude that the MOF is calling all the shots, however, is mistaken. Although the institutional structure of the MOF allows it to orchestrate private sector interests effectively, thus modifying the trend towards greater involvement of politicians, the MOF is following a political score it did not compose.

HISTORICAL BACKGROUND

Before World War II, Japan's financial system resembled the universal banking system still prevalent in continental Europe today. Banks and manufacturing concerns developed in close connection with banks owning corporate shares and handling a wide range of financial transactions, from lending and deposit taking to bond and equity underwriting. Securities firms existed, but they were left with the rather small niche of selling bonds and stocks to the public.

It was the U.S. Occupation (1945–1952) that conferred upon Japan a Glass-Steagall-equivalent, Section 65 of Japan's Securities Exchange Act of 1948, separating the banking and securities businesses. This action by a foreign power thus vested in the securities industry greater stature in the Japanese economy and political world. Predictably, the banking sector lobbied for the elimination of Section 65 upon the conclusion of the U.S. Occupation, but the securities firms reputedly made their survival worthwhile to the politicians who had control of their fate by plying them with stocks on the rise (Tatsuzawa 1985).

Despite the emergence of the securities firms as an important new group on the financial landscape, commercial banks remained central to the postwar economy. The prewar industrial combines *(zaibatsu)* were broken up by the Occupation officials, but in their place emerged *keiretsu*, bank-centered firm groupings that maintained varying degrees of intragroup cross share holdings and business relationships. Most large corporations maintained close ties with a main bank, typically the *keiretsu* bank, in addition to holding credit lines with several other banks. Japan's postwar economic growth was characterized by bank-dependent investment and high debt-equity ratios (Nakatani 1984).

In an exemption from the Antimonopoly Act, the Temporary Interest Rate Control Act of 1948 allowed banks to collect deposits at low interest rates, thereby guaranteeing banks a low cost of funds. The purported goal of this law was to induce banks to provide low interest rate loans to corporations. But Japan's so-called low interest rate policy has been overstated in much of the writing on Japan's industrial policy. In war-depleted Japan, banks had money, and corporations, which needed it for their ambitious investment plans, did not; this placed the bargaining power in the hands of the banks. Banks demanded compensating balances, commonly as high as 20 percent of the total loan, thereby sharply raising the effective rates of interest paid on corporate loans. If, for example, a corporation borrowed 100 million yen at 5 percent, 20 million yen was typically placed in an account bearing virtually no interest. The firm was actually paying 5 million yen in interest for the use of 80 million yen, making the effective interest rate 6.25 percent. With this device, banks were able to protect their profits in the face of the low interest rate policy (Horiuchi 1984).

A second important institutional feature benefited banks. In spite of Section 65's separation of banking and securities activities, banks succeeded in obstructing the development of the corporate bond market through their cartel-like *Kisaikai*, or Bond Arrangement Committee. Formed in 1933, the *Kisaikai* continued in the postwar period to set strict terms for domestically-issued corporate bonds, thereby enhancing banks' loan business (Nagatomi 1978).

It is reasonable to ask why, if deposit rates were so low, depositors did not switch to market-based financial instruments for a better return. The answer is that there were no such instruments because the MOF restrained competition by other institutions for bank deposits. The corporate bond market was small and sluggish, owing to the *Kisaikai's* control. Sometimes bank competitors did offer consumers investment alternatives. For example, in 1965, securities firms offered a corporate bond savings account, an instrument that would pass on to small savers the interest corporations paid for bond issues, minus the commission that went to the securities firms. This instrument proved to be popular because it was marketed in small denominations but bore a higher yield than bank deposits. Its success was brought to a halt by the MOF, however, in order to keep the securities and banking businesses in balance (Abe 1980).

Several changes in Japan's economic environment in recent decades have eroded banks' preeminence in the Japanese economy. First, slower economic growth, ushered in by the oil price hike of 1973, left its mark on every aspect of Japan's political economy; finance was no exception. In contrast with the heavy years of rapid growth when corporations had an insatiable appetite for bank loans to plow back into expansion plans and new projects, corporations were no longer willing to pay banks a high premium for a line of credit.

Second, despite Japan's slower growth, many firms had become international giants with excellent credit ratings in global financial markets. An increasing number of firms found they had access to more flexible and often cheaper funds from the Eurobond market. More cautious and eager to shave expenses in an era of slower growth, Japanese corporations began issuing bonds in the Euromarket with growing enthusiasm in the mid-1970s. In the early 1970s, the Euromarket accounted for a total of 1.7 percent of Japanese corporate financing. During the second half of the 1970s, that figure rose to

19.6 percent, and by 1984, it was 36.2 percent. As a portion of all Japanese corporate bonds issued, the Euromarket accounted for 51.9 percent in 1984 (Ichikawa 1986).

Japanese banks have fought to keep their best customers by cutting their spreads and phasing down compensating balances. Banks have also agreed to ease the conditions for domestic corporate bond issuance; the minimum capitalization requirements for issuing firms are gradually lowering, and a growing number of firms are permitted to issue debt without collateral. In exchange, banks have gained greater freedom to operate in the private placement market (Hoshi, Kashyap, and Sharfstein 1990).

Even as banks needed to make terms more attractive for borrowers, they faced depositors with stronger bargaining power. Large depositors, primarily corporations with cash and often excellent credit ratings, no longer blithely placed funds in low-yield accounts because they had discovered the opportunities of *zaitekku,* or financial management, in global markets. Now that firms feel freer to take their money elsewhere, banks are raising the yields on large deposits at the expense of their own profitability. To do otherwise would be to court extinction. Banks countered the burgeoning securities repo *(gensaki)* market, for example, with large denomination certificates of deposit (CDs) in 1979 that offered far better yields than regular bank accounts (Feldman 1985).

Small deposit deregulation has been much slower in coming because there have not been viable substitutes for savings accounts. Lacking alternative opportunities in the market place, small savers can, theoretically, demand that their political representatives change the rules of the market by, for example, abolishing the Temporary Interest Rate Control Act still in place after over four decades. But collective action theory explains why small savers do not take recourse to the political arena. This is a classic case in which the potential benefits of higher deposit yields are diffused across a wide swath of the electorate, giving no one a high per capita incentive to change the existing system, while the costs of such a change would be charged against the highly-organized commercial banks (Olson 1982).

To review briefly, the two changes in Japan's economy just noted were the growing bargaining leverage of bank borrowers and the growing leverage of at least large depositors. A third change that also disadvantaged banks was the sudden increased issuance of government bonds beginning in 1975 to battle the recession caused by oil price increases in 1973–1974. Since 1965, when the Japanese government first issued deficit bonds, banks had absorbed about 60 percent of the bonds issued. This posed no particular burden because the Bank of Japan repurchased the bonds from the banks as part of their supply of money in the system. After 1975, however, the quantities were too large for the Bank of Japan to reabsorb without fueling massive inflation; banks were incensed at having to hold the bonds to maturity (Noguchi 1987).

The MOF made several attempts to placate the banks, usually by adjusting accounting practices. Unappeased by such minor measures, the banks boycotted the government-bond placement syndicate and forced the MOF to relent. In the Banking Act of 1982, the MOF allowed banks to do what heretofore only securities firms were permitted to do under the Securities Exchange Act: sell government bonds to the public, trade government bonds for customers, and deal for their own account in government bonds to profit on price fluctuations. For the first time since the early postwar reforms, the MOF redrew the lines dividing the banking and securities businesses (Rosenbluth 1989).

The MOF made this sort of subsequent adjustment when establishing a commercial paper market in November 1987. Commercial papers are, in the United States, unsecured, negotiable notes with a fixed, but typically short, maturity (30 to 270 days) agreed upon by issuer and investor (Schaede 1988). Banks had long resisted the establishment of a commercial paper market in Japan, despite increasing corporate demand, because it would compete directly with their short-term loan business. And since commercial paper was treated as a security in the United States and the Euromarket, the securities industry would profit at the banks' expense by underwriting the instrument in Japan. Once corporations found a way around the banks by issuing commercial paper in foreign markets, however, the banks were ready for a compromise. The MOF struck a bargain between the banks and securities firms by defining commercial paper as a promissory note, thus avoiding the legal issue of whether banks could underwrite corporate securities. This enables both banks and securities firms to underwrite commercial paper in Japan (Litt 1989).

The deregulation of interest rates has continued steadily and gradually. By April 1991, all deposits less than 500,000 yen were technically free of interest rate restrictions. Deposits of this size (a little over $3,700 at an exchange rate of 130 yen to the dollar) were well within reach of the average Japanese household. Of some consolation to banks is the fact that the rates on money market certificates (MMCs) are set at a fixed spread over the rate on bank CDs, lest small banks be unable to compete. Nonetheless, the process of deregulation of retail-level interest rates has sharply raised the cost of funds particularly for small banks, since they had been sheltered as long as the rates only on large denomination deposits had been freed.

The MOF finds itself in an uncomfortable situation. It continues to be responsible for the protection of small banks, on the one hand, and it is accountable for the stability of an increasingly exposed financial system, on the other. The postwar history of Japanese banking regulation suggests that the MOF will continue to walk the tight line, encouraging mergers when it can, but will be unable to force a major overhaul of the system.

THE POLITICS OF REGULATION AND
THE JAPANESE INSTITUTIONAL CONTEXT

Before examining specific cases of financial regulatory change, we need to take a closer look at the players in Japanese financial politics, what their motivations are, and how they interact.

The Bureaucrats

Let us first consider the bureaucrats. A bureaucrat, maximizing his personal success, will behave in a variety of ways depending on who is assessing his performance. In Japan, what constitutes a bureaucrat's success is determined largely by the bureaucracy itself. In the MOF in particular, a bureaucrat stays with his agency for his entire career with a view to moving up the ladder before parachuting into a comfortable private sector job upon retirement (Calder 1989). Only the minister and one vice-minister are political appointees, and their job is largely one of coordinating policies with the rest of the Cabinet when necessary.

Given this sort of immediate chain of command, a MOF official's job proceeds most smoothly, and hence his chances of success are best, when politicians stay out, allowing the MOF to preside over the delicate balancing of interests, and second, when the financial institutions believe the MOF can enforce the compromises over which it presides. Unlike William Niskanen, I am arguing that a bureaucracy tries to maximize its jurisdiction only when its more important goal, ease of regulation, is also attained (Niskanen 1971). In fact, the MOF will voluntarily cut back its territory in some cases to avoid politicization or unenforceability.

Because the MOF is a single institution, it is able to forge decisions that take into account its various parts. The highest court of appeal, as it were, is within the MOF itself. Consider, by contrast, the United States, which has a Federal Reserve Board, twelve regional Federal Reserve Banks, the Securities Exchange Commission, the Department of the Treasury and its Comptroller of the Currency, the Federal Deposit Insurance Corporation, and, until recently, the Federal Savings and Loan Deposit Insurance Corporation, not to mention the state agencies that regulate state-chartered banks. Lacking interbureau coordinating mechanisms, differences among these many, diverse institutions are settled by politicians, the courts, or, by default, the market place (Peltzman 1965). Japan's Ministry of Finance is the equivalent of all these American administrative bodies rolled into one entity.

To borrow a metaphor from George Stigler, the "price" the MOF bureaucrat charges for regulation varies according to what other interests the MOF must weigh (1971). The price can range from virtually nothing, if the group bearing the cost of regulation is a dormant public, to a costly compromise with another tightly-organized interest group. That MOF is one entity with an encompassing jurisdiction enables it to preside over a wider range of compromises than is possible in a fragmented regulatory system such as that of the United States. But even the MOF, with its wide authority, is accountable to the politicians and must set its "price" in accordance with the will of the political representatives, lest it subject itself to unwanted political intrusion. What do the politicians want?

The Politicians

A politician may strive for a variety of goals, such as gaining status within the party or even achieving a particular policy objective. But because he first must get elected each time his term is at an end, he must maximize his chances for reelection subject to these other interests. And because reelection forces him to be concerned with his net support, he will not champion a cause, for whatever sum of campaign money or number of votes, if he would lose more potential support from a disgruntled party than he gained from the beneficiaries of his efforts. If, on the other hand, the interest group's only opponent is an unaware, unorganized public, the politician will likely attempt to increase his support by using regulation to give favors.

The Liberal Democratic Party (LDP) has influence over the MOF by virtue of its potential for intervening on behalf of aggrieved groups in the financial sector. But the LDP would rather delegate to the MOF delicate balancing operations between Japanese banks and their rivals, the securities houses, since the LDP would forfeit money and/or votes, on balance, if it favored one over the other. Phrased differently, banks and securities firms would prefer for the MOF to preside over compromises between them since the alternative is an expensive, upwardly spiraling competition for preferential treatment from the LDP.

The Courts

Another potential actor in financial politics is the judicial system. Indeed, readers familiar with the financial regulatory process in the

United States know that the courts are probably the central actors in U.S. banking regulation. In Japan, the role of the courts is remarkable principally for its absence.

In the United States, as in Japan and, for that matter, in any representative democracy, political representatives prefer to delegate problem-solving that vexes one important constituency or another. Given America's fragmented bureaucracy, however, even if Congress passes the buck, the buck cannot stop there in the vast number of cases that concern two or more regulatory bodies. Many issues are, therefore, settled in the marketplace or, if either of the competing groups is dissatisfied with that arena, before the courts.

In U.S. banking regulation, for example, each time the Federal Reserve permits commercial banks to slightly advance into the securities business, the Securities Industry Association challenges the regulation in the courts (Karr 1979; Adams 1982). Neither the Republican nor the Democratic Party has been willing to legislate against either commercial or investment banks in the ongoing competition between the two groups of financial institutions. Therefore, the courts rather than the bureaucrats or politicians have set the pace for the erosion of the Glass-Steagall Act (Reinecke 1989). This will likely continue to be the case until or unless commercial banking profits lag behind investment banking profits to such an extent that the politicians feel politically justified in picking favorites. They could hide behind plenty of rhetoric about shoring up an important industry in the face of the global competitive challenge.

Japanese courts hardly figure at all into the financial regulatory process. The primary reason is that the MOF's jurisdiction encompasses both the banking and securities industries as well as most other kinds of financial institutions. There are few disputes that cannot be handled by the MOF itself. Second, even if financial institutions were inclined to challenge the MOF by way of the courts, the administrative courts in Japan are reluctant to hear cases that concern the relationship between a ministry and an industry under the ministry's jurisdiction (Haley 1986). The courts have taken themselves out of the running as a major actor in Japanese financial regulation.

The Regulated Groups

The Japanese financial system comprises several different kinds of banks, ranging from twelve city banks, seven trust banks, and three large long-term credit banks to over one hundred regional banks and even more credit associations, credit unions, and agricultural cooperatives, as well as over two hundred securities firms (Feldman 1985; Cargill and Royama 1987; Suzuki 1985). The groups we are primarily concerned with here are the large, competitive banks represented by their peak organizations, the City Bank Roundtable *(Toshi Ginko Konwakai)* and the National Federation of Bankers' Associations *(Zenkoku Ginko Kyokai)*, and the large, competitive securities firms led by the "Big Four" securities houses: Nomura, Daiwa, Nikko, and Yamaichi.

From unequal points of origin shortly after World War II, the banking and securities industries have become interest groups of roughly equal political strength. Banks, individually and as a group, contribute more reported political campaign funds to the LDP than the securities firms. They are consistently among the top three corporate contributors. But untold sums make their way into politicians' pockets from the securities firms through the practice of stock price ramping (Repeta 1984).

CASE STUDIES IN FINANCIAL POLICY MAKING

Bureaucratic Preemptive Balancing: Bank Entry into Securities Activities

As was noted earlier, the MOF has resolved without LDP intervention disputes over the extent to which banks would be allowed to participate in securities activities. Although the Banking Bureau and Securities Bureau each leaned toward the position of the sector it regulated, they finally reached a compromise solution. Failure to do so would have incited either the banks, the securities firms, or both to invite politicians to overrule the MOF in their favor. The LDP, in any case, would not intervene, uninvited and uncompensated, because it would bring no net gain in campaign contributions.

Once the MOF provided a solution, the banks and securities firms were unwilling to pay huge sums to the LDP because the MOF's equilibrating service had a lower price tag. If the Banking Bureau and Securities Bureau were institutionally discrete, and, thus, lacking incentive to settle the issue in house, the banks and securities firms would surely have taken their cases to the politicians for resolution.

Disclosure: The Case of Unwanted Regulation

The MOF's desire has always been to have a strong, highly concentrated financial sector. It would be easier to regulate and less likely to produce panics and scandals that invite political intrusion. But political reality has dictated otherwise. Bank profits have been under strain with the trend, in recent decades, away from corporate dependence on bank loans, and numerous small banks have fallen into serious trouble. Instead of allowing weak financial institutions to go bankrupt, the MOF has often had to shore up politically influential, small banks with loans and to arrange bank mergers when possible (Nakajima 1979).

In 1981, as part of the new Banking Act mentioned earlier, the MOF attempted to tighten up bank disclosure rules in hopes of utilizing market forces to consolidate small financial institutions. The MOF felt that more stringent disclosure requirements and greater public exposure of bad loans would force weak banks to acquiesce to the MOF's merger plans.

The banks fought back. They launched a political campaign with the LDP to roll back the tightened disclosure requirements, and they succeeded. The two LDP Policy Affairs Research Council committees that deal with finance, the Finance Committee *(Zaisei Bukai)*, and Financial Affairs Research Committee *(Kinyu Mondai Chosakai)* met jointly and deleted in toto the MOF's chosen disclosure provision before submitting the Banking Act bill to the Diet for approval (Rosenbluth 1989).

Retail Banking: Fragmentation of Regulatory Jurisdiction

In retail banking, we confront what, at the least, appears to be a deviation from the pattern of the previous two cases, in which rule changes reflected the interests of the financial institutions themselves. Small borrowers and depositors do not have easy access to competitive foreign financial services. Domestic financial institutions should, therefore, have no incentive to compete for the patronage of small customers.

But in fact, they do. In Japan, the Ministry of Posts and Telecommunications (MPT), not the MOF, operates the largest bank in Japan, indeed the world. More than 100 trillion yen in deposits makes the postal savings system larger in terms of assets than the five largest city banks combined.

Perhaps even more important is the postal system's political power. Nearly 20,000 local notables, located in villages and communities all over Japan, are MPT-appointed postmasters, many having inherited the title from fathers and grandfathers. These postmasters are paid on a commission basis to market the postal savings instruments and insurance plans. They also are reputed to weild considerable vote-gathering power for sympathetic LDP politicians at election time. While this sort of political machine is less potent in Japan today than it was about a decade ago, and even less effective in urban than in rural districts, risk-averse politicians prefer not to cross the commissioned postmasters if at all possible (Johnson 1989).

The MPT keeps LDP politicians favorably disposed toward its operations through the electoral support of the commissioned post officers and through the political campaign contributions from telecommunications companies under MPT jurisdiction. The ongoing struggle between the Ministry of International Trade and Industry (MITI) and the MPT for jurisdiction over the telecommunications industry has been told well elsewhere and need not detain us here (Johnson 1989). The MPT has also done battle with the MOF for authority over setting interest rates.

Since the Postal Ministry (then the *Ekitei Ryo*) was established in 1873 with independent authority over postal savings interest rates, the MOF has attempted to integrate the postal interest rates into the rest of the financial system, but the Postal Ministry has persistently defended its turf. Known in Japan as the Hundred Years' War, this jurisdictional squabble has now outlived a century and is still raging.

Free from the Temporary Interest Rate Control Act that limits competition for deposits among banks, the postal savings system offers an instrument with slightly higher yields. This bete noir of the private banks, the *teigaku chokin*, is a 10-year fixed-amount savings deposit with biannual compounded interest and free withdrawal without penalty after six months. Banks cry foul, claiming that no institution concerned with its bottom line could offer such a generous savings instrument, and that the MPT subsidizes the postal savings system from its profitable postal services as a way of paying off the commissioned postmasters. The available evidence is inconclusive as to the basis for these accusations, but it certainly is true that many small banks would go under if they had to engage in an open competition with the postal savings system.

Unlike the competition between the banking and securities industries that pits the MOF's Banking Bureau against the Securities Bureau, the struggle between the MPT/postal savings system, on the one hand, and the MOF and private banks on the other, lacks an administrative mechanism to resolve the problem short of politicization. Politicians necessarily become involved because there is no other overarching institution to which they can delegate this sort of dispute.

After years of pulling and hauling and political maneuvering on both sides, the MOF and MPT finally agreed in the 1980s to a compromise solution: the MPT would still control the interest rates of the postal savings system, but both banks and the postal savings system would offer an identical higher yield savings account beginning in June 1989. This money market certificate (MMC) would require a 3 million yen (roughly $23,000 at 130 yen to the dollar) minimum deposit, and its interest rate would be set at a fixed spread from banks' certificates of deposits and government bonds (*Shukan Asahi* 1989).

Banks were by no means overjoyed by this resolution of the interest rate dispute. Higher yield, small-denomination accounts would raise their cost of funds. They wanted the MOF to enforce a lower interest rate ceiling on the postal savings system. But they got the best they could hope for, given the political clout of the MPT and the commissioned postmasters, because the outcome did avert unbridled competition for deposits. The MPT, in exchange for its side of the compromise, was granted a slightly larger percentage of the postal savings funds, from 2 to 4 percent, that it could invest on its own without handing over to the MOF's Fiscal and Investment Loan Program (Johnson 1978; Calder 1988).

That small savers have gained higher yields on their deposits was clearly not the result of consumer awareness and activism, but a by-product of a territorial squabble between two ministries fully unable to protect their clients. The key factor producing a different outcome from what we might have expected in Japanese finance is, therefore, jurisdictional fragmentation, not some sort of grass-roots campaign.

In addition to Japan's own small savers, a second group has also benefited from the higher yields on small savings deposits: foreign banks. Some foreign banking operations in Japan predate World War II, but all seventy-four foreign banks have a combined share of less than 3 percent of the Japanese loan market, a level that has persisted for decades (Pauly 1988). The thorniest problem for foreign banks has been the Temporary Interest Rate Control Act, which provides established domestic banks with a wealth of low-cost funds with which to make low-cost loans (if necessary), whereas foreign banks, lacking the name recognition to attract a large number of small deposits, must rely on the more expensive interbank market for funds. The more Japanese banks must pay for their deposits, the greater is the competitive advantage for foreign banks.

JAPANESE POLITICS

As the primary administrative agency overseeing the activities of the financial sector, the MOF is certainly involved in policy formulation and implementation. But as we have seen, the Ministry of Finance does not dictate its wishes to the financial sector. We must not mistake an active state for a strong one.

Bureaucratic performance, the MOF's highest goal, depends in large measure on bank compliance because politicians are always available as a last resort for the regulated parties. Hence, it is the political cost that sets the bureaucratic price for dispute settlement.

As long as small banks are powerful in local districts, and as long as the postal network continues to operate as a powerful local vote gathering machine, streamlining the Japanese financial system remains a distant goal for the MOF. An example of unfulfilled aspirations in another administrative agency is the MITI and its relationship to small business. Although MITI would prefer to preside over globally competitive industries, the LDP compels it to enforce legislation protecting small businesses from the encroachment of large conglomerates (Calder 1988).

If small banks and small businesses have demonstrated their political clout, individual consumers of financial services remain as politically unorganized as ever. As we have seen, higher yields on small-denomination deposits were not the result of political pressure from the public. Politicians brokered an interministerial battle between the MOF and MPT to prevent an all-out skirmish for deposits that would have crippled the banks. Establishing higher, but capped, interest rates was the second best solution for the banks and an inadvertent windfall for savers and foreign banks.

The MOF continues to protect banks in a number of ways in the name of guaranteeing the integrity of the banking system. Granted, depositors in Japan have never lost their bank savings in the postwar era due to bank failure, but the still relatively low yields on savings accounts are a high, forced premium depositors pay for safety. The small depositor could be protected by other means, such as strict balance sheet requirements or better deposit insurance. The rhetoric of "depositor protection" continues to disguise bank protection.

Despite the formidable lobbying power of interest groups, overtly protective regulation is, at least hypothetically, vulnerable to censure from political entrepreneurs who are not allied to the special interests that seek regulation for their own purposes (Noll 1983). Why do not ambitious politicians in the Liberal Democratic Party or in the opposition parties attempt to incite the silent voters to depose long-standing vested interests? After all, if strong leadership helped consumers of financial services to overcome their free rider problem, vast numbers would reward the reformers at the polls.

The short answer is that the LDP, which since 1955 has been the only party with the Diet majority necessary to formulate national policy, imposes strict voting discipline on its Diet members to prevent would-be mavericks from capitalizing on potential voter dissatisfaction with established policies. As in all parliamentary democracies, the LDP rank and file accepts strict voting discipline because the Party leadership controls the allocation of Party and Cabinet posts, and because a vote of no confidence against the leadership would mean they would all have to recontest their seats in another election.

The more complete answer requires a look at Japan's rather unique electoral system to understand why the opposition parties have not formulated electoral strategies and won elections on the basis of pro-consumer, pro-taxpayer platforms. Members of Japan's Lower House are elected from a multimember district system in which each voter has a single nontransferable vote (SNTV). Because the LDP must run several candidates against each other in most districts in order to retain a Lower House majority, LDP candidates must campaign on the basis of personal attributes and constituency services rather than on the basis of broad-based issues (Curtis 1971). This electoral system and the LDP's factional adaptation to it produce, in other words, patronage-based, rather than issue-based, political campaign strategies. The LDP will retain its majority in the Lower House as long as its candidates are able to satisfy (or promise to satisfy, in the case of new candidates) their constituencies on the basis of favors that distract attention from broader-based consumer and taxpayer issues (McCubbins and Rosenbluth 1990).

This electoral system only minimizes, but does not obliterate entirely, the political salience of broad-based issues. The opposition parties can and do score well electorally when they succeed in raising enough public concern about LDP policies to overshadow the LDP's constituency services. One example of genuine entrepreneurship by the opposition was over the loan shark problem that had begun to receive splashy news coverage in 1981. Taking advantage of public anger over reports of suicides because of inability to repay loans and of hired gangsters harassing overdue borrowers, the Japan Socialist Party and the Democratic Socialist Party launched a widely publicized campaign to lower the legal ceiling on the interest rate for consumer loans from the existing level of 109.5 percent. Despite heavy lobbying of the LDP by the consumer loan industry, the LDP had to give in to the opposition, lest it lose support of the aroused public. The Diet passed a law lowering the interest rate ceiling to 40 percent, hardly a bonanza for small borrowers, but enough to remove the spotlight of public concern (*Kinyu Zaisei Jijo* 1981).

Under the charismatic leadership of Takako Doi and with the help of the Recruit scandal, sexual improprieties of prominent LDP politicians, and the unpopular sales tax, the Japan Socialist Party fared significantly better in the Upper House election in July 1989 and the Lower House election in February 1990 than it had for decades. The LDP's loss of a majority in the Upper House somewhat crimps its ability to formulate and implement policy with only token concessions to the opposition. But the electoral system for the Lower House will continue to assist the LDP in retaining its majority there. Broadly-based public concerns still fare poorly in Japan's political system.

CONCLUSION

Japan's economic success is often attributed to its savvy adaptation to a changing global environment. The case of financial deregulation demonstrates that this adaptation was not part of a bureaucratic master plan but was the result of a government responsive to the interests of well-organized producers—in this case, producers of financial services. Financial deregulation in Japan reflects the interests of the same financial institutions that sought regulation in the first place. The changing economic environment in which the financial institutions operate has forced them to relinquish some protection in order to compete with institutions in markets beyond the Ministry of Finance's reach.

Some Japan observers have expected to see greater involvement of politicians as Japan's economy becomes more interlocked with the world economy. This has indeed been the case where internationally salient issues fall across the jurisdictions of two or more ministries, as in the telecommunications tug-of-war between the MPT and MITI (Johnson 1989). But financial deregulation has not been wholly politicized in Japan because the MOF balances competing interests under its jurisdiction in anticipation of political interference. The salient factor for the likelihood of politicization is the scope of bureaucratic jurisdiction, not internationalization. In the ongoing competition between the banks and the securities firms, the regulatory/deregulatory process gives them back at least part of what they lose in the market place. The MOF, following political cues, is redrawing the boundaries between these two industries to allow banks gradual entry into the more lucrative securities business. The MOF will continue this anticipatory balancing for the forseeable future since not only the MOF but also the financial institutions and the politicians find it in their interests.

CHAPTER 4

Imperatives of Development and the Formation of Social Policy: East Asia's Newly Industrialized Countries

Frederic C. Deyo

Beginning in the 1930s and 1940s, social development policy in much of the Third World has been powerfully driven by extra bureaucratic political forces. This is perhaps especially true in Argentina, Brazil, Mexico, and elsewhere in Latin America, which, therefore, provides a useful contrast to the experience of East Asia's Newly Industrializing Countries (NICs). In some instances, social development policy in Latin America was preemptive and anticipatory, as under Cardeñas in Mexico. In other cases, it was in reaction to existing political opposition and pressure, as in Brazil in the early 1960s and Chile in the early 1970s. Often, where such opposition severely threatened economic growth and the interests of economic elites, it was met by repression rather than by accommodative social policy reforms. In most cases, pursuit of a capital intensive, exclusionary, and inequality-generating development strategy (Evans 1989) heightened the incompatibility between economic and social policies, thus creating powerful currents of political and class conflict.

East Asian export-oriented industrialization, by contrast, has been associated with less severe distributive conflict, a consequence in part of weaker political organization of the popular sector, but also because of a greater compatibility between social policy and the developmental strategy favored by state elites.

The extent of this compatibility, in fact, increased over time. During the 1960s and early 1970s, pursuit of a development strategy based on cheap labor and light industry did eventuate in political conflict centering on such issues as wages and collective bargaining practices. Often, such conflicts, as well as the larger political contests in which they were embedded, were met by repression. However, as state development strategies were redirected to shifting the East Asian economies away from reliance on simple labor-intensive export manufacturing to higher value-added manufacturing and services, positive social policy which might enhance the skill and productivity of labor was seen as an ever more critical component of development policy itself. Thus, development policy in East Asian NICs has encouraged increasing support for expansive social policy. And where emergent political pressures have urged even more rapid movement in this direction, as in South Korea and Taiwan in the late 1980s, political responses have favored accommodation over repression.

This chapter documents this increasingly close relationship between economic and social policy in East Asia, showing that temporal change in social policy is closely related to evolutionary changes in economic strategy, relating particularly to efforts at economic restructuring during the 1970s. It is further argued that cross national variation in social policy among the East Asian NICs is explained in part by corresponding differences in the developmental roles of states and in the nature of the employment systems through which these countries have sought to wed domestic labor to the requirements of export-oriented industrialization.

MAJOR COMPONENTS OF SOCIAL POLICY

At the most general level, social policy refers here to state policies, practices, and institutions which directly influence the economic welfare and security of popular sector groups (farmers, workers, middle classes, and the like). Such policy has four major aspects. First, social policy is embedded in economic development policy insofar as economic policy has intended welfare consequences or reflects implicit or explicit socioeconomic priorities. Second, social policy includes incomes policy, that assemblage of measures which influence wages and benefits in both public and private sectors.

Third, social policy relates to direct government provision for social welfare, in part through public services and subsidies that benefit major social sectors. Subsidized health, public housing, education, child care, subsidized foodstuffs, public transportation, and welfare payments and public assistance programs fall into this category typically referred to as the social wage. Finally, the state may influence income security through pension schemes, disability and health insurance, unemployment insurance, and other measures typically included in social security systems. These schemes may apply to government workers, or they may be mandated for private sector firms. In the latter case, there may be substantial variation in the extent of state financing.

The following discussion provides an overview of East Asian social policy, first during the early period of export-oriented industrialization of the 1960s and early 1970s, and then during more recent years of economic restructuring. In each case, characteristics of social policy are related to development policy, the developmental role of the state, and employment systems.

EXPORT-ORIENTED INDUSTRIALIZATION: THE EARLY PHASE

At the very outset of East Asian policy reforms which ushered in the export-led industrialization strategy of the 1960s, it was recognized that political stability and legitimacy depended in large measure on a reduction in existing high levels of unemployment and enhancement of wages and standard of living. Acceptance of the need to adopt a strategy to achieve these ends, coupled with an absence of significant nonlabor agricultural, mineral, or other economic resources, encouraged an emphasis on light, labor-intensive manufacturing which might generate quick gains in employment. The success of this policy is seen in rapid declines in unemployment in these countries, eventuating, in fact, in growing labor shortages by the 1970s. Indeed, the need to expand employment was cited in support of more generally restrictive social policy in other areas. This is especially true for incomes policy.

During this early phase of export-led development, global competitiveness of East Asia's manufactured exports was based in part on cheap, productive labor. This consideration, along with a further determination to prevent early wage gains from restraining employment growth, implied a low-wage policy extending well into the 1970s. This imperative was met in Hong Kong by continuing immigration of cheap labor from the Chinese mainland. In Singapore and South Korea, by contrast, wage restraint invoked direct wage controls. Beginning in 1968, the Singapore government singled out pioneer industries (labor-intensive export industries promoted by the government) as free from any obligation to negotiate pay levels above government recommended minima. And from 1973, wage controls were formalized through the issuance of annual wage guidelines by the National Wages Council (NWC). Until 1979, these guidelines held wage gains to levels below productivity increases. Similarly, South Korea's Economic Planning Board issued yearly wage recommendations which held wage gains to a fixed percentage of inflation and

productivity gains. And in Taiwan, trade unions were generally prohibited from pressing for large wage increases.

This shared restrictive incomes policy was accompanied by greater
diversity in the nature and severity of state controls over trade
unions, as well as in levels of state provision for social wage and
social security. The following section describes these latter differences and shows their relationship to development strategy and to
variation in employment systems and in the developmental roles of
states.

At the outset of export-led development in South Korea, high unemployment levels sufficed to maintain low wages. Subsequent upward
wage pressures were contained by progressively tougher political
controls. Labor militancy increased over the 1960s, culminating in
protracted strikes against foreign firms in 1968 and 1969. Starting
with enactment of 1969 legislation curtailing strikes against foreign
firms or firms deemed important to the national economy, collective
action was increasingly circumscribed, especially after promulgation
of the Yushin Constitution of 1973.

In South Korea, wage compression and union controls were paralleled by very restrictive social wage and social security policy (Park
1975). Low government expenditures for education, social welfare
and security, health, and housing, in turn, reflected a single-minded
commitment to rapid, state-induced industrialization at whatever
social cost necessary. A major exception to this production first approach relates to provision, under the 1963 Social Security Act, of
pension, medical, and other benefits for the civil service, military,
and school teachers (Chang 1985). Indeed, a substantial portion of
total government social insurance and welfare expenditures have
targeted this politically important category of workers. Beyond this
protected segment of the work force, social insurance provision for
private sector workers has been uneven and minimal. The only major
legislation in this area, a national pension insurance plan enacted in
1973, was not implemented until 1988.

The vicious cycle of repression and protest which issued from early
coercive responses to demands for improved social policy was eventually to contribute to the political crisis and democratic opening of
the mid-1980s. In the shorter term, however, repression sufficed to
scuttle demands for higher wages, increased social expenditures,
and fuller provision for social insurance. In addition, repressive
labor policies buttressed the economic power of employers, who in
most cases were able freely to evade even those few protective labor
laws the government did enact.

Export-oriented development in Taiwan relied as strongly on low
wages as in South Korea, but a low-wage policy in Taiwan relied

much less on state repression. The key to understanding this difference in labor regimes is to be found in characteristics of industrial
structure and employment systems. Industrial development in Taiwan
centered more than elsewhere on elaborate subcontracting networks
among small and medium-sized family firms. These firms, embedded
as they were in the rich associational life of local communities, provided workers with a modicum of security against economic depri-
vation, albeit at very low wages. Enterprise paternalism, given further
encouragement under national legislation mandating a number of
employment benefits, greatly enhanced the power of employers. As in
Korea, government workers in Taiwan enjoy broad, although shallow,
social security benefits. Private sector legislation, however, went
far beyond that in South Korea. Under the Labor Insurance Act of
1958, as subsequently amended, employers are required to provide
death benefits, disability insurance, severance payments, and pensions for workers (International Commercial Bank of China 1983).
While government expenditure under this law is very limited, the
government does help finance social insurance for self-employed
persons under a voluntary insurance program (Chan 1985).

Enterprise paternalism encouraged by the government, along
with preemptive political controls imposed under martial law at the
outset of Kuomintang rule in Taiwan, eroded social pressure for
enhanced social policy. But despite this lack of political and union
pressure, Taiwan adopted a more proactive social policy than that
in South Korea. In part, this difference may be explained by the
Kuomintang's desire to achieve political legitimacy in its new insular
home and, thus, to avoid the political catastrophy it had suffered on
the mainland. In part, too, however, promotion of enterprise paternalism encouraged economic growth by fostering labor discipline
and enterprise loyalty. We will return to the developmental implications of paternalism below.

In Singapore, as in South Korea, wage constraint during this early
period was paralleled by extensive state controls over trade unions.
In the 1960s, such controls included detention of oppositional union
leaders, deregistration of many unions, and in 1968, introduction of
legislation which established a ceiling on permissible benefits and
greatly enhanced the power of employers in collective bargaining.
These measures were supplemented by both yearly wage guidelines,
noted above, and a system of mandatory industrial arbitration.

If labor controls grew ever more repressive in South Korea, they
moved in a different, more corporatist direction in Singapore. Starting in the early 1970s, the ruling People's Action Party (PAP) supported
the development of a comprehensive, powerful, government-controlled
national union federation, the National Trades Union Congress,

which subsequently became an important instrument of development
policy. Union officials, who also occupied high level government
positions, came to play leading roles in campaigns to promote wage
restraint, increased productivity, and labor-management cooperation.

Singapore's public housing program, even more ambitious than
that in Hong Kong, is the PAP's proudest accomplishment. By the
late 1980s, it accommodated over 80 percent of the total population.
In addition, the PAP instituted a comprehensive national pension
plan, the Central Provident Fund (CPF) and an extensive public health
service. In part, these social programs were products of early political
conflicts as the PAP sought to outmaneuver powerful leftist opposition in the newly independent republic. Having said this, however,
one must note that these apparently politically-driven welfare policies had important developmental outcomes as well. The CPF, for
example, has comprised a major source of finance for many government infrastructural projects. The magnitude of this pension fund,
along with the massive savings mobilized by the government Postal
Savings Bank, together go far in explaining Singapore's extraordinary
national savings rate of 41 percent, the highest in the world. It will be
suggested below that public housing has similarly important developmental consequences.

Hong Kong's continued immigrant flow along with a very weak
labor movement (Deyo 1989) fostered continuance of a labor-intensive
development approach far longer than that elsewhere, despite a
general absence of extensive labor controls to maintain low wages.
Structural factors, in part, explain the nonemergence of effective
labor opposition to immigration policy or to generally restructive
social policy in other areas. While a large and dynamic sector of
small family firms provided a parallel to the Taiwanese pattern of
enterprise paternalism (albeit without government-mandated benefits), the concommitant growth of large-scale factory employment
defined an important departure from the Taiwanese pattern. In these
factories, employment of low-skilled persons, many of them immigrants and young women, at very low wages provided not only a
ready pool of cheap, politically vulnerable workers, but also encouraged reliance on a highly proletarianized, transitory labor force
which presented little challenge to employers or to the colonial government to adopt social insurance or welfare protection for workers
(Deyo 1989; Henderson 1989; Chai 1990). This weakness of organized
labor, along with a determination on the part of the government to
intervene only minimally in the colonial economy, has encouraged a
continuing reluctance to introduce private sector social insurance
legislation. The colonial government of Hong Kong has established
a comprehensive social insurance scheme, covering severance, ill-

ness, and retirement for civil service workers (Hong Kong 1989). But unlike Singapore, Hong Kong lacks a public social insurance program despite growing but disorganized pressure for establishment of a colony-wide provident fund (Chow 1985).

The major exception to this lack of proactive social policy is Hong Kong's massive public housing program. While this ambitious program may, in part, be explained by continuing waves of immigrants from the mainland and a corresponding need to accommodate their housing needs, the political weakness of this group, alongside a more general political insulation of the colonial regime from popular sector groups, would seem to require a more persuasive account of so massive a public undertaking. One possibility is that here, as in Singapore, public housing has had positive developmental consequences which have been recognized and exploited by Hong Kong's more generally noninterventionist government.

Castells (1984a), in his discussion of Hong Kong's development, and Salaff (1988), referring to Singapore, argue that public housing has provided an important indirect stimulus to industrialization. Such housing resulted first in the elimination of informal sector nonwage work in traditional local communities which were displaced by such housing, while, at the same time, forcing newly housed families, and especially women, to enter the work force for the first time to earn wages for rent and other necessities. Beyond this impetus to workforce expansion, public housing also permitted the clearing of squatter settlements to make way for commercial and industrial development (Castells 1984b), while, at the same time, attracting and accommodating light industry complexes which draw their work force largely from the local population of housing residents. Such complexes provide employment for many women whose household duties would otherwise preclude travel to more distant work. Finally, subsidized public housing acts as a wage subsidy for employers by holding down the cost of living (Henderson 1989; Schiffer 1991). In these ways, proactive social policy has encouraged industrial development.

ECONOMIC RESTRUCTURING AND DIVERGENT SOCIAL POLICY

Growing labor shortages and increased wage pressure in the 1970s, along with growing protectionism in core economies of Europe and the United States, posed well-known threats to continued export expansion among the East Asian NICs. An earlier crisis of import substitution eventuated in a convergence on generally restrictive social policy in support of light industry-based export manufacturing. By contrast, this new crisis precipitated more divergent responses.

Growing wage pressures were, in some instances, met by heightened efforts at simple containment. South Korea and, to a lesser extent, Taiwan maintained low-wage policies through the 1970s. Given far greater oppositional militancy in South Korea than in Taiwan, Korea's low-wage policy led to greater repression through the 1970s and early 1980s. It should be noted that this repression was more effective during earlier years when U.S. backing for anti-Communist regimes was most assured, and became less effective during the late 1970s with the diminution of this external support for the regime.

In part, increasing repression was a product of new policies that encouraged the rapid development of heavy industries such as automobile manufacturing and shipbuilding. These industries tended to concentrate workers in large factories and compressed working-class residential zones, thus facilitating union organization and collective action. In the short term, repression sufficed to keep production and labor costs down and to resist expansion of social benefits. In the longer term, however, labor militancy culminated in the protracted strike wave of 1987–1988 and subsequent rapid wage gains by workers. Here, as in the other countries, and irrespective of type of political regime, unremitting market pressures pushed wages far above those prevailing in other developing countries. By the mid-1970s, it was clear that the only long-term solution was to restructure into higher value-added economic activities, whether in manufacturing or other sectors, in order to accommodate increased wage costs. Import liberalization, partly the result of external political demands, added further pressure for increased productivity and efficiency. Economic growth somewhat reduced this cost-based pressure through an enhanced domestic market for both consumer and producer goods, but export markets remained critical for continued growth.

Economic restructuring in manufacturing required substantial new investments not only in physical capital but also in expanded and upgraded education and training programs. Equally important, economic restructuring encouraged the development, particularly in Taiwan and Singapore, of more paternalistic employment systems through which to encourage greater workforce stability, better morale, and heightened enterprise loyalty in order to enhance productivity and returns on investments in worker training.

Singapore, unlike South Korea and Taiwan, reversed this earlier low-wage policy, seeking instead to preempt slow upward wage adjustment and an inevitable loss of international wage competitiveness by actively promoting wage increases, starting in 1979, in order to discourage further investment in low-skill, labor-intensive manufacturing. It is important to recognize that this new wage policy, which boosted wages by over 50 percent during 1979–1981, was grounded less in welfare considerations than in economic restructuring policies.

Table 4.1
Social Expenditures in the East Asian NICs as a Percentage of Total
Government Expenditures

Country	Year	%	Year	%
South Korea	1980	26.6	1987	29.1
Taiwan	1981	27.7	1988	30.5
Singapore	1980	30.6	1987	38.2
Hong Kong	1980	50.2	1987	53.1

Sources: United Nations Economic and Social Commission for Asia and the Pacific, 1988, *Statistical Yearbook for Asia and the Pacific,* Bangkok: United Nations; Republic of China, 1990, *Statistical Yearbook,* Taipei.

The growing compatibility of a more expansive incomes policy and economic growth, recognized first in Singapore, is paralleled in other areas of social policy as well. Table 4.1 shows changes in levels of social expenditures for education, health, social security and welfare, and housing and community services, as a percentage of total government expenditures.

This rough indicator of government policy priorities shows substantial increases in social expenditures in all four countries during the 1980s. The greater overall social expenditures in the two city-states of Singapore and Hong Kong largely reflect the far higher levels of urbanization there than in South Korea or Taiwan, and the greater attendant need for government provision of social services.

A disaggregation of these changing expenditures into more specific program components permits a fuller understanding of changing social policy. Table 4.2 breaks total social expenditures into functional budgetary categories.

These data provide a starting point for developing a social policy profile for the East Asian NICs. As compared with South Korea, Taiwan stands out here in its relatively lower outlays for education and health services, and its greater emphasis on social security and welfare. Similarly, Hong Kong's stronger commitment to welfare and housing contrasts with Singapore's greater stress on education.

Singapore's dramatic changes in expenditure during the 1980s require a note of explanation. First, the reduced expenditure for housing is explained by completion, by the 1980s, of the mammoth public

Table 4.2
Major Categories of Social Expenditure as a Percentage of Total Social Expenditures

Country	Year	Education	Social Security and Welfare	Health	Housing and Community Services
South	1980	64.4	23.9	4.6	7.1
Korea	1987	62.5	22.5	9.0	6.1
Taiwan	1981	42.2	46.5	5.8	5.5
	1988	47.2	40.9	5.3	6.6
Singapore	1980	47.8	4.4	22.7	25.1
	1985	62.7	4.6	18.8	13.9
Hong	1980	30.6	8.8	15.0	45.6
Kong	1987	34.4	11.5	18.2	35.9

Sources: United Nations Economic and Social Commission for Asia and the Pacific, 1988, *Statistical Yearbook for Asia and the Pacific,* Bangkok: United Nations; Republic of China, 1990, *Statistical Yearbook,* Taipei.

housing projects for which this city-state is so well known. Singapore's escalating educational expenditures have been directed to expanded vocational and technical training, at secondary and tertiary levels and in separate training institutes, as an essential instrument of state efforts to promote industrialization. Similarly, Singapore's low social welfare expenditures, in part, reflect comprehensive welfare programs for workers provided by trade unions closely allied with the ruling People's Action Party.

Singapore and South Korea present a more developmental, and less welfare-oriented profile of social expenditure than do Taiwan or Hong Kong, a finding that is congruent with more general differences in the degree of developmental intervention in these four countries.

The findings also point to an overall proportional displacement of expenditures on social welfare, housing, and community services by increased developmental spending on education and health in all four countries during this period of economic restructuring. But this is not to imply that social security and welfare programs necessarily undercut or compete with economic development goals. Indeed, the opposite argument, that such programs are supportive of growth, becomes ever more persuasive in the period of restructuring. It was noted that public housing already played an important economic role in Singapore and Hong Kong during earlier years. More recently, the stability of the work force and its loyalty to enterprises were increasingly sought by employers to support gains in productivity and returns on new training programs. This, in turn, led to enterprise-level welfare and social security programs mandated by the state, and these programs became ever more important for continued industrial transformation.

Hong Kong's continued access to cheap immigrant labor has encouraged a continuance of proletarian employment systems. In the absence of a national pension system, only about 14 percent of all workers were covered by pension and severance schemes as late as 1985. And although employers are now required to provide severance benefits for workers who have been employed at least ten years, many employers have been known to fire workers just before their tenth year of employment in order to avoid this legal obligation. While Hong Kong has ratified many ILO labor conventions concerning minimum working standards, enforcement in this area is similarly deficient (International Labour Office 1985).

In South Korea, a transition from state repression to paternalism has been precluded by the extreme hostility and volatility in labor relations. It is true that a national pension insurance plan, originally enacted in 1973, was finally implemented in 1988 in the context of political crisis. But coverage during the first phase of implementation extends to only 4.4 million workers. Similarly limited is coverage under the 1983 Industrial Injury Compensation Insurance Act, which provides medical coverage for work-related injuries. This and other worker welfare programs are contributory in nature, thus avoiding large government expenditures (Chang 1985). In fact, over one-half of all social welfare expenditures are privately financed. In addition, given inadequate public enforcement and widespread employer violation of newly mandated social insurance requirements, nominal workforce coverage greatly exaggerates actual coverage. Finally, South Korea has yet to ratify most ILO conventions relating to worker rights and welfare (International Social Security Association 1989).

Quite different is the situation in Taiwan and Singapore, where enterprise paternalism has been actively encouraged as an instrument of restructuring. Taiwan's enterprise paternalism was, in fact, well-adapted to the requirements of restructuring, insofar as workers were already closely bound to the fate of their companies through a range of economic and noneconomic sanctions and obligations. A continuing liberalization in state development policy over the 1970s and 1980s (Li 1989), and a corresponding dependence for growth on the continued vitality of small firms, built on this strong system of

paternalistic employment. Indeed, earlier social insurance requirements that had been mandated for local employers were further expanded after the mid-1970s and especially under the 1984 Labor
Standards Law, which requires employers to provide pension and
severance benefits, thus encouraging further enterprise paternalism
(Liu 1988).

In Singapore, large industry-wide unions were decentralized, and
house unions were encouraged. Many social insurance programs
were partially decentralized to firms. Educational and welfare programs, and, later, medical coverage, were to be administered by
firms. And severance pay and worker compensation programs are
now required of all employers. In these ways, the PAP emulated
Taiwanese efforts to enhance workforce stability and enterprise
loyalty. And here, as in Taiwan, such expanded government commitment to worker welfare and social security primarily has been driven
by the needs of evolving development policy rather than by the pressures of political dissent.

Recent expansion of social welfare and social security programs has
not been accompanied by the development of unemployment insurance plans. This exception to the more general pattern of expansionary
social policy may be understood by the fact that unemployment security would have undercut developmental goals during earlier years
when the discipline of the labor market was used to mobilize cheap
labor for export production and, more recently, as governments have
sought to bind workers ever more tightly by bonds of dependency to
their firms. One exception here is Taiwan, where a new Labor Insurance Act was established in 1979 to provide limited employment
insurance. But this program was indefinitely suspended "because of
low levels of unemployment" and, significantly, because it was felt it
would lead to "welfare dependency" (Chan 1985). Assistance to
Taiwan's unemployed remains confined to public assistance for the
very poor.

DISCUSSION: THE COMPATIBILITY OF SOCIAL
AND ECONOMIC DEVELOPMENT POLICY IN EAST ASIA

With the exceptions of Singapore in the early 1960s and South
Korea in the late 1980s, East Asian social policy has been more
strongly shaped by the developmental priorities of politically insulated states than by extra bureaucratic political forces as in Latin
America. Political autonomy, popular movements, and labor opposition have been related in the NICs to social organizational and
economic structural factors, on the one hand, or by political co-option
or repression, on the other.

Thus, political autonomy has largely been allied with proactive social policy. Indeed, in many instances, East Asian social policy has been far more progressive than that in other developing countries. The link between elite-guided economic development and decent social policy records, particularly during recent years, is, in part, explained by the nature of the development strategy. East Asian export-oriented industrialization has centered on the effective utilization of human resources. Under such circumstances, economic development has been energized by social policies that have subsidized wages, enhanced labor productivity, and encouraged training within firms. To this extent, economic development and proactive social policy have been mutually supportive.

The compatibility between social and economic development policy has greatly increased under economic restructuring. During the early period of development based on light industry, plentiful, low-wage labor provided the key to export expansion and economic growth. At that time, a clear incompatibility existed between some elements of social and economic policy. In particular, a repressive incomes policy, along with a reluctance to increase production costs by mandating company welfare programs, often necessitated strict political controls over labor. Nonetheless, even in this early period, expansionary social policy in other areas, such as housing, often supported, rather than undermined, industrial expansion.

The later shift to higher value-added industry greatly enhanced the degree of compatibility between social and economic development policy. Such increased compatibility related especially to the need for higher levels of skill and productivity in the context of declining unemployment and concomitant upward wage pressures. Most obvious is the productivity benefit derived from increased expenditures for education (especially vocational training) and health. Similarly, as industrial restructuring proceeded, incomes policy could be relaxed. And as workforce stabilization and enterprise loyalty were increasingly sought by employers as a precondition for increased investment in worker training, mandated enterprise-level social security benefits became ever more supportive of continued industrial transformation.

The extent of compatibility also varied according to the nature of the employment systems through which domestic labor was wedded to international capital, technology, and markets. For example, proletarian labor controls relied extensively on the power of labor markets to discipline workers, expecially during early industrialization; in this system, enhanced social wage and income security measures that might have sheltered workers from the discipline of labor markets were incompatible with economic expansion. By contrast, where labor controls relied to a greater extent on employer paternalism, social wage and income security measures were more compatible with economic policy.

It is clear, too, that the nature and extent of state guidance and intervention in the development process conditioned the extent to which simple compatibility between social and economic policy was reflected in enactment of social development measures. States whose governments systematically attempted to restructure their economies by directly influencing investment decisions were more prone to implement development-enhancing social measures. Less interventionist states, where economic growth was encouraged through more indirect means, tended to exhibit a looser correspondence between economic and social policy. Thus, the more interventionist states of South Korea and Singapore accorded greater social policy priority to education than community welfare than did Taiwan and Hong Kong during recent years of industrial restructuring. It should be noted, however, that large public expenditures on housing in Hong Kong, and on social security and welfare programs in Taiwan, also played important, if less direct, roles in economic development.

It finally may be noted that the recent, if tentative, democratization in South Korea and Taiwan may prove more enduring now than in the past. If earlier repression was based, at least in part, on the need to pursue exclusionary social policies in order to foster industrial growth, a greater compatibility of such policies with the developmental imperatives of restructuring offers greater latitude for political liberalization. This possibility is perhaps best demonstrated by recent events in South Korea. Following student and middle-class political agitation against military rule in the mid-1980s, free presidential elections were held in 1987. During subsequent months, a massive wave of strikes closed down important export industries across the country and led to rapid wage increases. During the next two years, emergent political pressures led to implementation of both a minimum wage and a national pension system, extension of medical insurance to the entire population, and, in 1990, a doubling of government expenditure for public housing. This accommodative government response to unprecedented political pressure stands in marked contrast to earlier coercive measures taken under less threatening circumstances. Clearly, the durability of democratic institutions in this charged political climate is uncertain. Indeed, there are some indications of a reversion to repression. Police have been used to break strikes, an important oppositional union movement has been banned, and there is growing middle-class fear of continued political instability and violence. On the other hand, there is a shared perception that a government crackdown now would be based largely on political considerations. The economic rationale relating to a need to maintain low production costs and export competitiveness, so often heard in former crises, has increasingly become a secondary issue in public debates.

ACKNOWLEDGMENTS

The author is indebted to Manuel Castells, Paul Evans, Jeffrey Henderson, Su-Hoon Lee, Minjoo Oh, Janet Salaff, Michael Shafer, and Richard Stubbs for helpful comments on an earlier draft of this chapter.

CHAPTER 5

Korea's Experience and Future Prospects of Economic Development

Taewon Kwack

In the relatively short period of twenty-five years, the economy of South Korea has transformed from a poor, primitive, agrarian economy to a dynamic industrial economy of upper middle-range income. The growth rate of per capita income during this period ranks among the highest in the world, along with other Asian NICs and Japan. In addition, equitable income distribution now seems to be a regional characteristic of Asian nations, and Korea has fared well in this respect.

Korea differs markedly, however, from other successful Asian NICs in that it has accumulated a large amount of foreign debt in the course of economic development. Unlike many other countries, however, she is overcoming her debt problem via successful economic growth and a trade balance surplus. The inflation problem also had been solved in the mid-1980s. Although inflation had not been as bad as in the Latin American economies, it was a constant threat to the Korean economy.

Economic growth has not equally satisfied all members of the society. And when it does not parallel comparable political and social development, economic growth can create tension or open conflict. Recent sociopolitical tension in Korea may be interpreted along these lines. In spite of the favorable economic performance, the public is not satisfied. Their demand for more political freedom and more equitable income distribution directly and indirectly initiated various social changes. Among them, the all-out labor strikes of the summer of 1987 and the resulting wage increases may affect the future course of economic development very significantly.

The objective of this chapter is to highlight key features of Korea's economic growth in the last twenty-five years and to evaluate the impact of recent socioeconomic changes on the future course of Korea's economic development. We will first briefly review the development policy and performance of recent decades. Then, we will identify and relate key factors in the successful growth of the economy. Finally, we will discuss recent socioeconomic development of the country and the impacts of such development on future economic growth.

A HISTORICAL OVERVIEW OF KOREA'S ECONOMIC POLICY AND PERFORMANCE

It is difficult to define precise stages of development, especially when the total period considered is relatively short. Korea's modern economic development can be conveniently divided into several distinctive stages because the economy had a very condensed development experience during its relatively short history of rapid growth. In this chapter, we will divide the period reviewed into four stages for explanatory convenience. These are: 1) Reconstruction (1950–1961), 2) Export-Oriented Industrialization (1962–1972), 3) Drive Toward Heavy and Chemical (HC) Industry (1973–1980), and 4) Liberalization (1980s).

Reconstruction (1950–1961)

The Korean War destroyed Korea's already weak industrial base to almost nothing. Scarcity of jobs, shortages in supply of basic consumption goods, and rampant inflation were the only abundant elements. Because of the extremely low level of income, the national savings rate did not exceed 5 percent, bringing the typical vicious circle of poverty; that is, low income level > low savings > low investment > low growth. In addition, policy-makers were inexperienced in planning and managing economic development, and they could not find a strategy to solve these problems. Industrial policy focused on import substitution in a few consumer and intermediate goods industries, such as flour milling and fertilizer manufacturing. The gap between investment and saving was largely filled by foreign aid. However, because of the small domestic market and the large capital requirements of the industrial investment projects, the policy of import substitution soon reached its limit. Agricultural land redistribution implemented during this period helped improve income distribution, but with the traditional capitalist class destroyed, the private sector could play only an insignificant role in the reconstruction of industry.

This period also marked a turnaround for education. Both in household and in public budgets, expenditure on education was a very high priority. Though the visible economic performance was poor (1953–1961 GNP growth rate: 3.7 percent; real per capita income growth rate: 0.7 percent), the educational investment in the 1950s became an essential element in pursuing the development strategy of the following decades.

Export-Oriented Industrialization (1962–1972)

The gospel of economic salvation preached by the military government that came into power in 1961 was a politically appealing one. The new government, however, was no better experienced in economic policy-making than its predecessors. Even worse, foreign aid, the lifeline of the Korean economy in the 1950s, was rapidly drying up, causing a drastic supply shortage and dramatic inflation in 1963 and 1964. The income level remained very low (United States, $82), and there was massive unemployment. Leaders of the military government, however, were wise enough to solicit advice from experts and foreign consultants in various fields. Korean economists educated in the United States, rare at the time, were fully used to map out a strategy and plans for economic development. The choice of an outward-looking development strategy through the export promotion of labor-intensive, light manufacturing products was a very natural one. At the time, 65 percent of the population was agrarian and growing at the high rate of 2.9 percent per annum. The supply of arable land was fixed, and the population density was high. The land was not endowed with any exploitable natural resources. The domestic market was very small because of the low income level. The only abundant resource was a disciplined and relatively well-educated labor force.

The period of the mid-1960s was a very important turning point in Korea's economic history. The philosophy of liberalization was applied in actual policy reforms already in this period. Before these reforms, the government tightly controlled major price variables such as the exchange rate and interest rates, and consequently, the corresponding resources were, in effect, rationed. In particular, the Korean currency (known as the won before the currency reform of 1962) had been kept overvalued, and the official interest rates were suppressed to a level far below that of the curb-market rate. The first reform was actualization of the foreign exchange rate (a drastic depreciation of the won). It was followed by a financial reform that raised the official deposit rate from 11 percent to 30 percent in 1965. In 1967, policy-makers introduced a so-called negative list system of import licensing, taking a big step toward the free-trade regime. The government also began to encourage the inflow of foreign capital. These price-correcting reforms aimed mainly to mobilize domestic savings and to promote exports. The government also provided various fiscal and financial incentives to the exporters.

Largely due to these reforms, the savings rate increased from 3.2 percent in 1965 to 14.5 percent in 1971. During the First Five-Year Economic Development Plan period (1962–1966), exports quadrupled, and the value of imports almost doubled. During the second plan period (1967–1971), exports again increased by about four times, and imports tripled. During the two five-year plan periods, fueled by the export expansion, the economy maintained a high average growth rate of 8.7 percent (6.9 percent in per capita), and the inflation rate remained at a relatively stable level from 1965.

Drive Toward Heavy and Chemical (HC) Industry (1973–1980)

The outward-oriented development strategy changed substantially in the 1970s. The focus shifted from labor-intensive export industries with the establishment of the Committee for Heavy and Chemical Industry (HCI) Development in 1973. The Korean government initiated such a shift in industrial development strategy for several reasons. Following two especially important events in the early 1970s, the policy-makers in Korea began to recognize the vulnerability of Korea to external shocks. One event was the opening of U.S.-China relations, which incurred the fear of a possible withdrawal of American troops. The other was the first oil crisis in 1973 and rising protectionism in the world market. Therefore, achieving self-sustenance in various fields, from food grain production to national defense, became one of the highest-priority national goals. Working toward this goal entailed launching many import-substitution projects. Selection of relatively less-developed heavy and chemical industries as potentials for import substitution was a natural one. The HCI sector also included most of the defense industries. In addition, Korean products were losing their price competitiveness in the international markets because other developing countries with cheaper labor began to enter labor-intensive manufacturing product markets. China's potential to enter the world market was even more threatening as a low-wage competitor.

To promote this strategy, the official interest rates were adjusted continually downward in spite of Korea's chronic inflation of the 1970s. Generous and targeted tax incentives were provided to investment projects in HC industries. Investment funds from domestic and foreign sources were directed to these sectors by the visible hand of the government, usually at an interest cost even less than the already low official rates.

Though the bold promotion of investment projects in the 1970s resulted in high growth (1972–1979 growth rate: 9.7 percent) and rapid capital accumulation, it exacted a substantial price from the Korean economy. For example, the easy-money policy and suppressed interest rate resulted in very high inflation, which most seriously afflicted the real estate market. The promotion of a self-sustenance strategy, ironically, resulted in heavy indebtedness. In a nutshell, the heavy industrialization policy in the 1970s, though it spawned quite a few successful projects, brought about various evils that included inflation, a worsening of income distribution, concentration of economic power, an increase in the foreign debt, and creation of many helpless production units in heavy industrial sectors. The second oil crisis revealed all the problems that had accumulated in the economy during the heavy industrialization period. With a negative growth rate, a big increase in current account deficit, and a hyperinflation of 39 percent, the year 1980 was the worst in Korea's modern economic history.

Liberalization (1980s)

Korean policy-makers in the early 1980s decided to respond to the economic crisis with stabilization efforts and liberalization strategies. To promote price stabilization, the government cut public spending drastically and controlled monetary growth very tightly. In 1984, for example, the governmental budget, including the salaries of civil servants, was frozen. The government also removed various direct and indirect subsidies, including various tax incentives to heavy industries and price subsidies to grain farmers. As a result, the overall fiscal deficit was reduced dramatically from 4 percent of GNP in 1981 to around 1 percent by the end of the decade. The growth rate in the money supply also dropped from an average of 30 percent in the late 1970s to about 10 to 15 percent in the mid-1980s. Thanks to Korea's tight monetary and fiscal policies, the inflation rate was drastically reduced, from about 39 percent, measured in WPI in 1980, to 4.7 percent in 1982, and less than 2 percent in 1985. The success of the Korean economy in controlling the spiral of inflation and infla-

Table 5.1
Historical Performance of the Korean Economy

	Growth Rates (Average, % per year)				Per Capita GNP (in Current US$)	GNP (Middle of the Period, in Current Price, %)				Current A/C Balance (in Million US$)
	Population	Economically Active Population	Real GNP	WPI		Investment	Saving	Exports	Imports	
1962-66	2.70	2.79	7.8	16.2	104	15.6	8.7	6.7	13.5	-237
1967-71	2.24	3.15	9.7	7.8	210	29.4	18.8	15.4	26.0	-2652
1972-76	1.74	4.16	10.1	19.2	523	22.9	20.5	29.5	41.9	-4904
1977-81	1.55	2.26	3.8	19.9	1,546	34.2	26.6	32.5	40.2	-15191
1982-86	1.43	1.14	8.2	0.9	2,012	30.3	27.1	43.5	44.9	-1899
1982	1.56	2.52	5.4	4.7	1,773	28.6	20.9	43.1	47.8	-2650
1983	1.53	0.32	11.9	0.2	1,914	29.9	25.3	41.4	44.4	-1606
1984	1.46	-0.95	8.4	0.7	2,044	31.9	27.9	44.0	46.1	-1373
1985	1.34	3.80	5.4	0.9	2,071	31.1	28.6	41.6	42.7	-887
1986	1.25	3.38	12.2	-2.2	2,296	30.2	33.0	47.6	43.5	4617
1962-86	1.87	2.85	8.6	11.9	-----	----	----	----	----	----

Source: Bank of Korea, *Economic Statistics Yearbook 1986*.

tionary expectations was a major achievement. Stabilization, thus, became a solid foundation for structural adjustment.

As an approach to remedy the structural difficulties, the government promoted liberalization in various areas of the economy. The first step toward a market economy was already taken in the mid-1960s when the exchange rate and the interest rates were adjusted to the market rates. In the 1970s, however, during the process of HC industrialization, the Korean government kept a strong grip on resource allocation. As the economy expanded and grew in complexity, the cost of governmental intervention and resource allocation caused serious imbalances and inefficiencies in the economy. Thus, a comprehensive liberalization program was undertaken in order to promote competition and to enhance the efficiency of the market mechanisms.

Domestically, for example, five government-owned commercial banks were privatized in the early 1980s. Administrative price controls were reduced or removed completely, and a new fair trade and antimonopoly law was enacted to encourage competition and prevent collusion among firms. Korea's more important reforms were enacted in the area of external transactions. Trade reforms involved the active liberalization of the domestic market according to a schedule announced in advance. The policy-makers made an effort to explain to the general public that, by permitting foreign competition through market liberalization, the competitiveness of domestic firms could be strengthened in the long run, and consumers, who bore the cost of industrial protection, could enjoy higher quality products at lower prices. At the same time, the targeting of strategic industries, which was much used as a tool to promote heavy industrialization in the 1970s, was discontinued. The system of preferential interest rates and financial facilities for specific industries was phased out in the early 1980s. Instead, Korea's industrial policy became focused on providing general support for labor-force training and investment in R&D.

Due to these adjustments and also to favorable external conditions, the economy regained its rapid rate of growth as well as its unprecedented balance of payment surpluses and low rates of inflation. The historical performance of the Korean economy is statistically summarized in Table 5.1.

KEY FACTORS EXPLAINING THE SUCCESSFUL ECONOMIC GROWTH

What major factors might explain Korea's successful economic growth in recent decades? On the demand side, the single most important element has been exports. The real growth rate of exports for 1960–1986 was 22.3 percent per year, while that of GNP was 8.0 percent. Thus, the Korean economic growth clearly was led by exports, and the term export-led growth is not off the mark in this sense. For exports to grow at a high rate, the production rate should also increase at a comparable speed, and the supply price should be kept low enough to maintain the competitiveness of exports. Therefore, on the demand side, we must look at the external conditions, including the expansion and structural changes of demand and competition in the world market. On the supply side, we must examine the growth of the factor input including their qualitative changes, relative price structure of production factors, progress in technology, incentives and subsidies, international supply conditions of major intermediate input, and structural changes of the overall production sector.

The role of the government is important in all aspects of the above, but it is especially important in the choice of strategy. Particularly in the early stages of development, the market is unable to choose the best "strategy." A simulation study by Kwack (1983) indicates that choosing the correct strategy is far more critical than choosing an efficient set of policy measures to implement the selected strategy. Export orientation is not always a better strategy than import substitution. In the Korean case, however, it is difficult to deny that the export-promotion strategy that was actually chosen was better than the other alternatives. Many benefits of the export-led growth strategy have been identified; to name some, economies of scale when the domestic market is small, less distorted relative price structure through the reflection of the international relative prices, better access to the developed technologies and quality standards, better access to foreign financial sources (by showing the capacity to service debt), and better access to high-quality capital goods and inexpensive intermediate goods (by being released from foreign exchange constraints). Even without most of the above benefits, the outward-oriented development strategy suited Korea better than the inward-looking strategy because the domestic market was too narrow and because the endowment of factors, including natural resources, was too imbalanced (Westphal 1981).

In the early 1960s, Korea was a typical labor surplus economy. The labor not only was abundant but also grew fast. Even today, after a rapid industrialization period of twenty-five years, labor is still a relatively abundant factor of production. In such an economy, labor is of so low a value that its theoretical market price (or social marginal productivity) is zero. Naturally, wages were very low in the early 1960s and still are compared to Western industrialized countries. In the export-oriented industrialization strategy, wage rate plays an important role in keeping the export goods competitive. Thus, the low absolute wage level contributed greatly to Korea's effective penetration into the world market. This is shown by the fact that, in the decade between 1963 and 1972, the factor ratio of labor to capital was roughly three to one. For the decade 1972–1982, however, capital investment had proportionally doubled, yielding a labor-capital ratio of two to one (Kim and Park 1985:61–62).

Combined with policies that limit the rights of labor, however, the low level of wage has invoked criticisms that Korea's export-promotion strategy has been based on a type of wage exploitation. Though low wages played a critical role in maintaining the competitiveness of Korean exports in international markets, the ethical connotation of the phrase "exploitation of labor" is incorrect. First, the wage rate and the unit labor cost have been increasing very rapidly because of policies that repress the price of capital. Second, the labor share of total income has been steadily increasing. Third, Korea's agricultural sector, which has served as a reservoir of labor, is still protected. In other words, society is paying a substantial cost (in terms of efficiency or welfare loss) in order to control the oversupply in the labor market and to prevent a fall in wages.

Interestingly, though the unit labor cost in Korea has been growing very rapidly in ratio to developed economies, Korean export has consistently maintained its price competitiveness. Dornbush and Park (1987) provide an explanation of this phenomenon. Import of new technology decreases the unit labor cost in the front line industries by raising productivity, and these industries emerge as new exporters. However, the wage level in these sectors increases as does the wage level of traditional sectors whose productivity is unchanged. Consequently, the unit labor cost of the traditional export industries rises, causing them to lose competitiveness in the export market. In this process, the average unit labor cost rises while the marginal industries' cost (front line industries) goes down. Thus, the apparent conflict between rapid rise in the average unit labor cost and the maintenance of export competitiveness is reconciled. This explanation is supported by the rapid upscale transformation of the composition of Korea's exports.

Education clearly played an important role in causing high growth of productivity. During the Japanese occupation, Korean citizens were severely disadvantaged in the educational system. In response, education became a major preoccupation since Korea's independence. Educational enrollment was already high in the early 1950s, and, as a result, the illiteracy ratio dropped rapidly. In the early stages of development, the workers who received at least a primary school education under the new educational system were a key factor in the success of export-oriented industrialization. They could read and follow instructions; they had discipline and an orientation toward achievement.

Table 5.2
Educational Enrollment Levels

	Secondary School (% of Age Group)		Higher Education (% of 20–24 Age Group)	
	1960	1983	1960	1983
Middle Income Countries				
Lower	10	16	3	12
Upper	20	55	4	14
Industrial Countries	64	85	16	37
Korea	27	89	5	24

Sources: World Bank, 1983, *World Development Report,* New York: Oxford; World Bank, 1986, *World Development Report,* New York: Oxford.

In the later stages, entrepreneurship and knowledge played an important role, spurred by strong, mostly private investment in human capital. The priority placed on education has increased over the years, since better educated workers are more highly paid and are accorded greater social status. Thus, higher education was an investment with high return and low risk at the time. Furthermore, because the traditional social structure and bondages were almost shattered by the drastic sociopolitical changes, any strongly motivated and intelligent young man, regardless of his family background, could attempt to achieve a highly rewarding life. The average length of education was 7.2 years in 1960, 9.3 years in 1970, and 10.3 years by 1980. Already in 1960, Korea exceeded the average for middle-income countries in high education enrollment levels. By 1983, the country approached the educational standards of industrialized countries, as indicated in Table 5.2.

The top college graduates assumed governmental posts, joined large companies, or pursued advanced academic degrees in foreign universities. Government officials and personnel of large corporations were sent to overseas educational institutions for more systematic training. Such manpower provided competent planning and managerial services that were essential in pursing an outward-looking strategy, both in private sectors and in public organizations.

Compared with the amount of resources poured into education,

R&D investment was relatively small. Investments in both R&D and human capital have long gestation periods before yielding returns. Private firms and the government simply could not pay too much attention to those long-run projects because there were always higher priority investment opportunities whenever investment funds were available. In addition, the society was unstable or its outlook uncertain, resulting in shortsighted decision-making. The case of education was different for the aforementioned reasons. On the demand side, because Korean firms could import foreign technology at relatively low costs, they could not foresee any coming bottleneck in research and development. R&D investment began to be emphasized rather recently. One of the most valuable resources Korea had was scientists who had been educated overseas. Because of the big gap between the technology needed at home and the knowledge they acquired in the advanced countries, however, Korea benefited relatively little in the earlier stages of development. The reversal of the so-called brain drain is recent.

About 20 percent of the past GNP growth is explained by the increase in capital input. In other words, growth of capital stock or investment has played an important role in Korea's economic growth. It also is very natural because Korea's growth accompanied rapid industrialization which required high investment.

Following the interest reform of 1965, the domestic savings rate increased rapidly; however, until recently, the investment rate was increasing at an even higher speed, resulting in a rather heavy reliance on foreign savings. Because the Korean economy has been capital scarce, it is natural that the domestic rate of return is much higher than in the world financial markets. However, except for the period of 1965–1971, the official domestic interest rate has been kept very low, and hence, the domestic capital market has been unable to function properly in allocating investment resources. As the major owner of commercial banks, the government exercised a powerful role in rationing funds until the financial liberalization in the 1980s. This practice peaked in the 1970s during the HC industry drive, and much inefficiency followed as mentioned earlier. The low interest rate policy kept the domestic investment demand at a high level, generating a large gap between investments and savings. This gap was filled by foreign funds.

A few features should be noted in the whole process. First, because of the high domestic real rate of return on capital (or in other words, abundant investment opportunities), inefficiencies generated by government intervention in the allocation of investment resources did not greatly effect Korea's growth. Second, the government officials were alert. The economy in the 1970s was managed by a group of top-quality technocrats. Third, despite the government's power, resources were not allocated solely at the discretion of the government or political elites. In the midst of government planning and intervention, the market played a very substantial role. For example, the government decided to allocate more resources to the export sector, but the market chose the composition of the export sector. This type of division of roles in resource allocation between the government and the market was quite helpful in reaching the second best solution when the market was not mature enough to play its role, especially in the area of dynamic resource allocation.

Fourth, an important factor that led the strategy of high borrowing/ high investment to success was domestic political stability. Largely because of the stability in domestic politics and relatively high probity of most Korean political and business leaders, the economy has not suffered seriously from capital flight. As long as the borrowed money was kept inside the country, because the economy had so many productive investment opportunities, it was prone to reap an acceptable return.

The foreign exchange rate policy and various financial and fiscal incentive policies also helped the outward-looking strategy to succeed. It is not as easy to evaluate the contributions of shifts in the exchange rate and various financial and fiscal incentives. Clearly, during the import-substitution phases (1950s and 1970s), the government adopted policies of overvaluation, whereas in the export-promotion phase (1960s) and in the liberalization stage (1980s), the exchange-rate policy was used to improve the balance of payments. Until very recently, plenty of incentives to export were given throughout all stages.

Finally, the world economic environment should be mentioned, especially with regard to the economic performance in the 1980s. Dornbush and Park (1987) argue that Korea (as well as other Asian NICs) was fortunate, compared with Latin American countries, during the second oil and interest rate shocks because the NICs had much less deterioration in terms of trade. In effect, the NICs were protected by differences in the structures of their economies since they were net importers of commodities. Korea also is more able to adjust to the shocks than Latin American countries, which also helps to explain the relative success of Korea, especially in recent years. All these factors combined to give Korea its high economic growth.

RECENT SOCIOECONOMIC CHANGES
AND FUTURE ECONOMIC PROSPECTS

The period since 1987 is interesting in many ways for Korea's development. In terms of economics, though greatly owing to the favorable external conditions, major chronic problems have been dramatically solved. Price stability, balance of payment surplus, and near full employment were realized simultaneously in this period. On the political side, too, Korea had a very dramatic event, the "June 20 Declaration," in which the ruling party promised drastic democratization. There was intense labor unrest following the announcement. Almost all companies in Korea faced fierce demonstrations and protests by workers. The industrial turmoil, however, suddenly settled down by the end of September. Except for the restless summer, the economy remained extremely stable and peaceful. The firms all recovered their pace in production and shipment, and foreign buyers again crowded to Seoul. In its wake, however, suddenly increased labor costs burden the economy and impel shifts toward much higher value added to production.

A few fundamental questions arise. What were the basic reasons for the massive labor disputes? Were the reasons economic or political? How could the disputes disappear so suddenly? Is this the solution to the problem, or are second and third waves coming? What impacts will these events have on the socioeconomic development of the country? Clearly these questions go beyond the scope of this chapter. Instead, we will focus on a key economic aspect of the issue: the change in the relative price of labor. The single most visible and definite effect of the labor turmoil was an increase in labor price. The average additional wage increase in the manufacturing sector after the 1987 increases was estimated to be between 5 and 10 percent. Such a sudden increase in the cost of labor has had impacts on domestic inflation, employment, income distribution, export competitiveness, and industrial structure.

Price stability, as mentioned earlier, was one of the most important achievements of the Korean economy in the 1980s. On account of the low-expected inflation, rapidly increasing liquidity through the foreign sector has been effectively absorbed by financial savings, not causing any serious threat to the price stability. The labor disputes, however, critically undermined faith in the price stability. In addition, the scheduled elections, according to past experience, were strongly associated with inflationary expectations. Unstable movements in the real estate market also were reported, reflecting the lowered level of confidence in price stability. Such reactions were not groundless. First of all, the wage increases were not directly caused by improvements in productivity. On the contrary, the breaking of the informal controls and the loosening of labor discipline may, at least in the short run, cause a drop in productivity in terms of both production amount and product quality. Noting that the labor share in the value added is about 47 percent, the 10-percentage point extra wage increase without any productivity growth will push costs up an estimated 4 to 5 percentage points. Of course, a considerable

Table 5.3
Relative Population Size by Age Cohorts (as of 1987)

Age Group	Male	Female
5 - 9	88.7	87.6
10 - 14	92.0	91.5
15 - 19	100.0	100.0
20 - 24	92.8	92.5
25 - 29	90.5	94.5

Source: Economic Planning Board.

portion will be absorbed by decreased business profits. The government will do its best to maintain the stability. Indeed, the new government was challenged to do so since its inauguration.

Domestic inflation would critically weaken Korea's export competitiveness. There has been tremendous pressure to appreciate the Korean won against the U.S. dollar. Under such a situation, it is difficult to make an optimistic projection of the export growth, which has depended so much on its price competitiveness. The traditional labor-intensive sectors will be hit most severely, of course. Therefore, this process will accelerate upward adjustments of the industrial structure toward more higher value-added production. Since exports require imports or intermediate goods and capital goods, curbing the export growth may not reduce the balance of surplus so sharply in the short run. Inflation, however, will lower the real rate of return on financial savings, and this effect in turn would pull down domestic savings, resulting in a decrease in the current account surplus.

The most critical issue that the Korean economy will face in the coming years is the unemployment problem. Table 5.3 shows a peculiar demographic structure of this country.

The size of the 15- to 19-year-old cohort stands out dramatically. This group has already begun to create disturbances in the labor market. In addition, because of the liberalizing trend in society, women's participation in the labor market is rapidly expanding. Until very recently, young women in Korea automatically retired the moment they got married. This tradition, however, has been disappearing at a dramatic rate. The college enrollment ratio jumped in the early 1980s, and, counting the compulsory military service period for men, the oversupply of college graduates in the recent boom years can be explained very well. In sum, even without the labor unrest of the late 1980s, providing sufficient jobs for new entrants in the labor market would still be the most important socioeconomic problem in the current decade. The rise in the cost of labor following the labor unrest reduced demand in the market. In the short run, business investment declined as the competitiveness in the export market dropped. Since labor-intensive sectors were most severely hit, a unit of new investment generated a smaller number of jobs. Even in capital-intensive sectors, because of the rise in the relative price of labor, the introduction of labor-saving technology has accelerated. This precocious substitution of capital for labor seems to be expedited by an increased psychological cost of labor. Those business persons who had seldom had such experiences discovered a new side of the workers. They found that the obedient, productive workers can, at any moment, turn out to be an untractable violent group of rebels. Their solution could be to minimize the number of workers.

Popular support for the labor movement was based partly on the belief that a wage increase would improve income distribution. For the longer term, however, such a belief may be unfounded. First, unemployment will be a real problem in the future as the above discussions imply. Since Korea does not yet have any unemployment compensation system, increase in unemployment could worsen the income distribution critically. Interestingly, the firms that settled wages at relatively higher increased rates were, in general, large corporations which had already been paying high wages. Second, the inflation stimulated mainly by the wage rise will aggravate inequalities in the distribution of wealth and income; this is because inflation is, in effect, a regressive tax. It is difficult to evaluate the net income distribution. It also is difficult to evaluate the net effect of the wage rate increase on income distribution, but clearly, such a wage increase in itself would not necessarily improve the equity of the national income distribution.

Finally, we can say a few words about industrial structure. We already mentioned the possibility of premature or excessive adjustment of the domestic industrial structure because of the rise in labor costs (excessive to the level at which the labor market clears). Because of labor market conditions, however, the government may be tempted to delay the schedule to remove agricultural protection. In this case, the dualistic structure of the economy would deepen and the problem of imbalance would become more serious. Conversely, the government may choose to direct more resources to the social development projects such as housing, social overhead capital formation, and social welfare programs.

Fortunately, the Korean government has appropriate programs

through which it can raise a substantial amount of funds in the coming years. In other words, expanding public expenditure for social development is quite feasible. Throwing this single stone carefully, the Korean economy can catch many birds: the surging demand for social welfare services would be considerably satisfied, trade balance surplus would be effectively reduced, employment would be increased and, in the long run, the Korean economy's structural dependence on export growth would be reduced.

CONCLUDING REMARKS

We have reviewed Korea's development since the 1950s and discussed a few key factors which might have contributed to its success. We also discussed the recent labor unrest and its implications for the economy.

For the economy to further mature, Korea must overcome numerous internal and external challenges. Too much uncertainty makes any projection about Korea's future course of development tenuous. In addition, the problems standing before Korea look gigantic. However, since political democratization and the Olympic Games have been carried out with relative success, the economy seems to be finding a more steady path to continued growth and increased political stability.

CHAPTER 6

The Social Foundations of Institutional Action: Argentina and South Korea in the Postwar Era

Miguel E. Korzeniewicz and
Roberto P. Korzeniewicz

Argentina and South Korea provide a striking contrast in trajectories of social and economic development among semi-industrialized countries in the postwar era. Over the last twenty years, GNP per capita has grown at an average yearly rate of 6.6 percent in South Korea, and of less than 0.5 percent in Argentina. Manufacturing in South Korea grew 21 percent between 1965 and 1973, and 11.5 percent between 1973 and 1984; in Argentina, manufacturing grew 4.6 percent during the first period, and actually declined 0.2 percent between 1973 and 1984. Total exports grew sevenfold in Argentina during 1970–1980, but close to twentyfold in South Korea (World Bank 1987). In short, while these indicators show Argentina to have sustained a consistent pattern of economic decline, South Korea is shown to have experienced high rates of economic growth. How can this striking divergence be best explained?

The role of the state, labor organizations, landowners, and industrialists in shaping national development policies has been the subject of intense debate in advanced, industrialized nations, but it has received less systematic attention in countries such as Argentina and South Korea. In this chapter, we argue that relations between labor, capital, and the state, along with the institutional consequences of these relations, have been a central factor accounting for the strong contrast observed in these trajectories. We have found that rapid economic growth in postwar South Korea was associated with the consolidation of a peculiar articulation between a strong state and an emerging industrial class. In Argentina, on the other hand, a consistent pattern of sectorial conflict has been associated with the persistent instability of institutions and macroeconomic policies. Thus, our study is concerned with the structural conditions that underlie policy-making, both at the level of the institutional behavior of "open" organizations and at the level of the social coalitions that promote or undermine policies.

Furthermore, we argue that timing was important in shaping the divergent trajectories of Argentina and South Korea. For example, it is easy enough to observe that the opportunities that policy-makers within each country faced at the level of the world market differed a great deal; these opportunities were bound in time and space. We show that these differences in timing had social consequences which limited and constrained the options available to state policy-makers at different points in time. We also argue that relational aspects should be considered as well; the divergent trajectories of Argentina and South Korea were not discrete and independent events but rather an outcome of processes shared in common.

This chapter has four sections. The first section contrasts the evolution of the agrarian class in each of the two countries. Second, we examine the most salient differences in the historical development of the industrial sector, focusing most closely on the relationship between the state and industrial entrepreneurs. In the third section, we review the major differences in the structure of the labor force and its impact upon labor organizations. For each of the three economic sectors, we have sought to identify the social context from which the most important sectoral institutions emerged and the most important channels of political action available for the purpose of achieving economic goals. Finally, we draw some conclusions regarding the relationship between social conflict and patterns of semiperipheral development.

The conclusions derived from this study are useful in illuminating, albeit in a tentative fashion, *problematiques* that are specific to semiperipheral, advanced developing nations. An analysis of the South Korean case also helps to understand issues associated with dynamic growth under a controlled and centralized political and social environment. An analysis of the Argentine case helps to identify themes associated with economic maturity and stagnation in a context of high politicization. A contrast of different state-market relations in the dynamic semiperipheral segment of the world economy may offer some original insights into key contemporary questions about social and economic development.

LANDOWNERS

One of the more immediate and lasting effects of the Japanese occupation of Korea was that it resulted in the weakening of the landed aristocracy and in the virtual destruction of Korea's system of social stratification. Japanese occupation had both a direct and indirect impact in the long-term organization of land tenure in South Korea. Its direct impact resulted from the appropriation of more than one-half of the total land by the Japanese colonial state. Its indirect impact involved the fact that Korean landlords depended upon their association with the colonial state to continue appropriating agricultural surplus from tenants. In the process, the landlords "became tainted by association with imperial rule" (Cummings 1987:54; Kim and Roemer 1979:3).

The clear association between land tenure and the colonial state facilitated the emergence of political pressures for land reform at the end of World War II (Choi 1985:4). These political pressures were further fed by the massive return of immigrants and refugees to South Korea. Tensions between North and South Korea made the threat of peasant uprisings and rural unrest in the South particularly sensitive for policy-makers and led to the formulation of plans for land reform (Hsiao 1986:12).

Initial steps toward land reform were carried out by North Korea during the war and occupation (Cummings 1987:66), but the first formal agrarian reform was carried out by the American Military Government (AMG) in 1948, when more than 90 percent of previously Japanese-owned land was distributed among South Korean peasants. The land reform, which was extended to large farms in 1949, reduced the average size of individual farms to less than 2.2 acres and eliminated almost all large farms. By 1959 only 0.3 percent of all farms exceeded seven acres in size, and 42 percent were 1.2 acres or less (Wade and Kim 1978:18).

The emerging structure of agrarian relations had several consequences. First, it deactivated a potentially strong social actor, effectively dissipating for decades to come all possibilities of the landowners achieving any significant measure of political power. Second, it made it easier for resources to be channeled from agriculture to industry. In part, many former landlords moved directly into industry and commerce because the bonds issued by the government in compensation for land reform could be cashed into stock of newly-created firms (Hamilton 1986). More importantly, the terms of exchange deteriorated in favor of industry during the 1960s, and this was facilitated by the limited political power of the small new farmers. Finally, small farms served as the basis for households providing wage labor to urban areas. On the one hand, this involved urban workers who viewed their presence in the wage labor market as a temporary condition. At the same time, wage labor supplemented rural household incomes, further diffusing a potential source of rural unrest.

In Argentina, landowners played a key role in the very formation of the modern economy and consolidation of the republic after the 1860s. While there has been considerable diversification of capital through the twentieth century, landowners and rural producers have continued to be identified, both by themselves as well as by other social classes, as supporting a separate set of political and economic interests.

This has had several important consequences. First, rural interests have continued to play a predominant political role, challenging state policies whenever the latter have promoted industry to the detriment of agricultural and livestock production. The political veto power of the agrarian sector lies in the high weight of livestock and agricultural exports within the balance of trade and the frequent need to rely upon these exports to correct deficits in the balance of payments.

This points to a second consequence: namely, the difficulties in transferring surplus from agriculture to industry, and the recurrence of stop-and-go cycles for much of the postwar period. During the upward phase of these cycles, the growth of industry leads to a deterioration of the balance of payments due to increased imports of capital goods and to stagnation in exports. Devaluations are carried out to stimulate rural exports and to reduce the level of imports by raising the value of foreign capital goods. This, in turn, dampens industrial activity and has a recessive effect upon the economic cycle. Eventually, the commercial balance of trade provides a new surplus of foreign revenues, increasing currency values in a context of inflation, and allowing for the industrial sector to recover ground vis-à-vis the export sector. In overall terms, these stop-and-go cycles have allowed industry to grow unevenly at best, providing an unstable environment for the growth of manufacturing.

A third consequence was that the rural sector was placed in an antagonistic relation vis-à-vis wage workers. Periodic devaluations undermined real wages by increasing the value of foodstuffs (at one time, both an export and a wage good). This intensified conflicts between labor and capital as well as between the industrial and export sectors. In time, these cycles involved self-enforcing mechanisms in social behavior: under pressure from exporters, fiscal policies accentuated recessionary tendencies in the downturn phase of the cycle; under pressures from organized labor and industrial entrepreneurs, they encouraged expansion during the upturn of the cycle. In this sense, the economic bottleneck was a political bottleneck, expressing shifts in the balance of power between different social classes.

Table 6.1
Origin of Industrial Capital in Korea, 1941 (%)

Japan-based Corporations	74
Japanese Residents in Korea	12
Government Corporations	12
Koreans	2
Total	100

Source: Jones, Leroy P. and IL Sakong, 1981, *Government, Business, and Entrepreneurship in Economic Development: The Korean Case,* p. 26, Harvard University Press: Cambridge.

INDUSTRIAL ENTREPRENEURS

Korean manufacturing firms grew substantially under Japanese occupation, particularly after 1935. Also, a large infrastructure was created, including communications and transportation. Overall, "colonial manufacturing growth in Korea, 1910–1940, averaged 10 percent per annum, and overall GNP growth was in the 4 percent range" (Cummings 1987:45). From 1910–1912 to 1939–1941, real value added in manufacturing grew more than 10 percent a year, and by 1936–1940, manufactured goods accounted for more than 40 percent of total exports (Westphal 1981:36).

The Japanese legacy alone does not explain the rapid growth of manufacturing firms in South Korea after the mid-1950s. After all, during the occupation, the bulk of output and large enterprise manufacturing were both controlled by Japanese firms. There were also few Korean technicians, and much of the heavy industry and economic infrastructure was located above the 38th parallel. Finally, the Korean War destroyed almost half of the manufacturing plants existing in 1949 (Kim and Roemer 1979:39). Table 6.1 shows the sources of industrial capital in Korea under the Japanese occupation.

Import-substituting industries were fostered after the mid-1950s by favorable state policies and a backlog of consumer demand (created during the war), at a time when potential investment funds were available through foreign aid (Lim 1985; Hamilton 1986:29–38). Although some industrial entrepreneurs were landlords and capitalists from the colonial period, most were either former employees of Japanese firms, who took over these firms after confiscation of the properties, or newcomers to entrepreneurial activity (Lim 1985:104–

105). From the outset, state policies encouraged the emergence and development of large corporate conglomerates, the *chaebol*. The first generation of *chaebol* formed in the 1950s and included firms such as Samsung, Lucky, and Ssangyong. The growth and consolidation of these manufacturing firms during the 1950s was inextricably linked to the interaction between domestic policies and flows of foreign capital, particularly foreign aid. United States leverage, through aid funds and privatization, acted as the catalyst in the formation of a capitalist class (Cheng 1986:13).

Access to sources of capital during the Rhee regime was based substantially upon political connections and the corruption of bureaucrats. Kim indicates that through "bribery, graft, and corruption, a limited number of elite entrepreneurs was able to rise rapidly as the leaders of large monopoly combinations" (1979:78). The military coup that brought Park to power in 1961 led to significant changes in the relation between capitalist entrepreneurs and the state. Under the Rhee regime, both political and bureaucratic contacts had been necessary to have market access; after 1961, the Park regime emphasized more bureaucratic contacts. Thus, a new set of economic incentives was given to entrepreneurs, establishing a new, formal institutional framework for the linkage of the state and the private sector (Haggard 1983).

The Park regime was clearly committed to fostering economic development on the basis of a "flexible and pragmatic" relationship between capital and the state (Westphal 1981:35). However, the Park regime was initially antagonistic vis-à-vis important groups of entrepreneurs accused of corruption, and this initial confrontation allowed the military regime to take the initiative in creating political conditions that asserted state leadership and guidance towards the private sector. The state in South Korea had an important influence in the development of manufacturing firms through four major mechanisms: direct economic policies fostering the formation of an incipient industrial sector, establishing long-term stable macroeconomic policies, regulating competition from multinational corporations, and regulating the financial sector.

During the 1960s, the Park regime pursued a strategy of inducing firms to shift from import-substituting to export-led manufacturing. This strategy was implemented through a combination of currency devaluations, increased access to capital imports, and tariffs and indirect tax exemptions for exporters. It also included the reduction of incentives for socially unprofitable import substitution (Westphal 1981:35). A second major shift in economic policy occurred during the 1970s, when it became increasingly difficult to maintain a competitive position in light manufacturing and state policy-makers pushed

Table 6.2
Chaebol in the Korean Economy, 1975

Number of Chaebol	Chaebol Value Added as Cumulative Percentage	
	GDP	Manufacturing GDP
5	5.1	14.5
10	7.7	21.8
20	10.6	30.2
46	13.4	36.7

Source: Jones, Leroy P. and IL Sakong, 1981, *Government, Business, and Entrepreneurship in Economic Development: The Korean Case*, p. 266, Harvard University Press: Cambridge.

for a move towards heavy, capital-intensive industries (Haggard and Cheng 1987:118).

Through the 1960s and 1970s, large economic conglomerates diversified their operations, from a concentration in food and textiles to heavy, capital-intensive industries such as electronics, automobiles, machinery, and shipbuilding. These transformations in the *chaebol* were accompanied by a process of concentration and centralization of Korean firms. Table 6.2 shows some aspects of this process of concentration.

While intrasectoral conflict in South Korea has been much less apparent than in the Latin American cases, the cleavages between large and small and medium firms increased through the 1970s. The speed of the vertical integration of large industrial corporations can be attributed to domestic financial incentives and to a more active role for foreign capital. The result of this concentration has been an "industrial dualism," where large corporations control the market and medium and small firms play a minor role (Kim 1985:82–84).

The most important consequence of these arrangements is that the state effectively has been the predominant partner in its alliance with large industrial firms. As indicated by Koo, "Because of its strength in determining the structure of the development coalition, the Korean state had power to select domestic capitalists for inclusion in the alliance and to determine how fast they could accumulate" (1986). From this perspective, development strategies can be interpreted as a means to achieve political goals. For example, industrialization was originally viewed as a means for nation-building itself (Hsiao 1986:14). And in the 1970s, security concerns on the part of the military and political challenges to the Park regime were the most significant factors leading toward state promotion of heavy, capital industries in the 1970s (Haggard and Cheng 1987:123). In turn, economic performance provided a considerable basis to generate political legitimacy among a large segment of the population (Cheng 1986:58).

Patterns of state intervention are also significant in two important respects. First, it has served to contain competitive pressures within industrial capital itself. For example, South Korean entrepreneurs have not been subjected to direct competitive pressures from multinational corporations (Koo 1986; Hamilton 1986). In fact, the state acted as intermediary between domestic firms and international commercial lenders (Haggard and Cheng 1987:112). Foreign capital complemented, rather than stunted, the formation of local capital and entrepreneurs. The state undertook an active role in channeling U.S. foreign aid into the early development of industrial enterprises, while the presence of multinational corporations in South Korea was effectively screened, regulated, and administered by the state.

Second, state action was most significant in preventing financial capital from becoming a competing economic force in relation to strategic goals around manufacturing. Since the 1960s, the government engaged in a clear policy of separating financial capital from industrial capital, including the seizure of several commercial private banks in the aftermath of the illicit wealth scandals of the late 1950s. In the 1960s, industrial entrepreneurs continued to experience a lack of autonomous control over financial resources. The *chaebol* continued to rely upon government-controlled credit institutions. The state also established controls over interest rates to increase private savings and simultaneously to discourage unproductive use of bank credit (Kim and Roemer 1979:45). Thus, the state forced entrepreneurs to abandon lucrative arbitrage for a then uncertain future in the risky export business (Haggard and Cheng 1987:117).

This brief examination of the main features of South Korean industrial development in the postwar era reveals two crucial characteristics that have shaped the institutional role of industrial entrepreneurs. First, economic development in South Korea has been inextricably tied to the growth and consolidation of giant corporations, or *chaebol*. Such a concentration of economic power translates itself into political power. "Size and power beget influence which in turn produces privileged access to credit, foreign exchange, and government's complicity" (Jones and Sakong 1981:259). The fact that economic and political power are combined in one entity allows the *chaebol* to act much more coherently and efficiently, not only in the pursuit of economic goals, but also in the attainment of political means to meet these goals.

Second, *chaebol* have enjoyed a remarkable insulation from the kind of competitive pressures that have undermined the consolidation of an industrial class in other developing countries. The agrarian bourgeois was severely weakened in the late 1940s, and financial capital was regulated by the state and, thus, barred from becoming a competing economic force. U.S. foreign aid was channeled into the early development of *chaebol*, and the presence of multinational firms in the local economy was effectively screened, regulated, and administered by the South Korean state. In essence, the South Korean capitalist class has not been subjected to competitive pressures from multinational corporations (Koo 1986:16). Only in the area of direct foreign loans are large South Korean firms subject to the same economic and political vulnerabilities as entrepreneurs in other developing countries. However, the recent repayment performance of South Korean firms is impressive when contrasted to that of most Latin American countries (*Asian Wall Street Journal*, June 1, 1987; *Far Eastern Economic Review*, March 12, 1987).

To summarize, the most distinctive institutional implication of postwar economic development in South Korea is the formation of large, powerful conglomerates engaged in a cooperative relationship with the state. These corporations are insulated from competing social groups, are sustained by a legitimizing ideology, and are active in state policies through the financing of political leaders.

In Argentina, the development of manufacturing in the late nineteenth century was closely tied to the spectacular growth of agricultural exports. A high-wage labor force tied to export activities resulted in a large domestic market that attracted investments in manufacturing. Originally confined to light manufactures and transportation equipment, industry grew faster and in new sectors after 1914 and during the 1920s, when firms from the United States and continental Europe made large industrial investments in an effort to counter the favorable tariff treatment granted to British imports.

The success of the agrarian-based development model prevented the emergence of serious social and political challenges. Agrarian interests wielded the greatest political power throughout this period, while Argentine industrialists lacked effective political channels. The most important entrepreneurial organization, the Argentine Industrial Union (UIA), was founded in 1887. Between the 1880s and the 1930s, the UIA's demands consisted of requests to the government for higher levels of protectionism, tariffs on foreign manufactured goods, and the alteration or derogation of specific labor laws. The most important political action carried out by the UIA in this period consisted of a large meeting that took place in 1933 to express opposition to the terms of the "Roca-Runciman Treaty" that had been signed that year by the governments of Argentina and Great Britain. This treaty established quotas of Argentine beef exports in exchange for British manufactures and was denounced as contrary to the interests of autonomous development in Argentina (Alberti and Castiglioni 1985:8–9). The hegemony of the agrarian sector continued, even in the midst of the crisis of the 1930s, as bilateral arrangements allowed for a swift recovery.

State policies were directed toward promoting manufacturing in the midst of World War II, when the military came to act in the belief that state institutions, and especially the traditional political parties, had become too outmoded to deal effectively with both changes in the interstate system and the newly emerging balance of social forces. The Argentine military embarked in the launching of ambitious industrial programs, including the production of steel and modern armaments. There is evidence that the military presence in the economy effectively preempted entrepreneurial initiatives in key sectors, but there is also evidence that a number of state enterprises created and administered by the military in the 1930s and 1940s were privatized after 1955 (Alberti and Castiglioni 1985:10).

As part of the new development strategy subsequently implemented in the 1940s and early 1950s by the Peronist administrations, state policies pursued industrial growth by providing easy-term loans to entrepreneurs, protecting the domestic market with tariffs, stimulating consumer demand by increasing wages, and redistributing income from rural exporters to the urban sectors. This development strategy provided a basis for the formation of a broad political coalition, involving urban and rural workers, industrial entrepreneurs, small farmers, and the middle class.

This alliance proved effective during the 1940s, but limitations were reached in the 1950s. First, Peronist state policies ran into a balance-of-trade bottleneck that constrained the economy for years to come. Second, there were difficulties in increasing productivity in industrial firms, at a time when there was rising competition. Altogether, these pressures weakened the alliance and provided political space for opposition to develop.

In this period, a second generation of industrialists emerged in Argentina. In the late 1940s, the General Economic Confederation (CGE) and the Confederation of Industry (CI) were formed. These organizations claimed to represent the interests of small and medium firms and also firms from the country's hinterland, as opposed to the large, Buenos Aires-based firms that comprised the majority of the UIA's membership. In 1946, the UIA was intervened and closed. In 1955, after the ouster of favorable context, the Peronist government that came to power in 1973 sought to construct an updated version of the populist coalition that had been effective in promoting an earlier stage of import-substitution development in the 1940s and 1950s. The CGE was revitalized, a social pact was signed among labor, business, and government leaders, and a five-year plan was formed that targeted heavy industries and manufactured exports as the basis of economic growth.

The regime that took power in 1976 was explicitly committed to compensating one sector of the economy (agrarian exports), at the expense of industry, and to deregulate and expand the former's diversification into the emerging financial sector. The goals of the economic policies of the period were to make industry more efficient (and, therefore, more competitive in world markets), to concentrate power in the hands of a few large corporations that would combine industrial, agrarian, and financial interests (structures reminiscent of the *chaebol*), and to expand and diversify financial markets themselves. These policies failed as soundly as the ones that had been adopted in 1973, leading to stagnant economic growth, high rates of inflation, and a process of deindustrialization. In summary, through the 1970s, Argentina not only failed to diversify its industrial structure and the composition of its imports, but actually *declined* in its industrial capacity between 1975 and 1983.

The decline of industrial activities has been accompanied by a diversification of financial markets. Inflationary pressures in the late 1960s and 1970s were themselves an expression of acute social conflict. Speculation developed as a defensive mechanism on the part of capitalist entrepreneurs, in effect diverting financial resources away from productive investments, and the state did little to contain its impact upon economic activities. Over the last decade, the financial sector in Argentina has grown out of all proportion to the size of the economy, due to widespread speculation, high real interest rates, and the influx of foreign capital. In addition, there was a strong segmentation of both financial institutions and financial markets on the basis of access to international sources of capital. In contrast to the South Korean case, the state in Argentina today has little control over financial speculation, and this has become perhaps the most important obstacle to the implementation of development strategies.

There are two clear patterns that emerge from this examination of the institutional behavior of the entrepreneurial sector in Argentina. First, the interests and goals of the private sector have had to contend with a high differentiation of institutional forces. The number and strength of these sectors has remained constant or increased as a result of the relatively long trajectory of economic development. In contrast to South Korea, where large industrial corporations and a relatively strong state were able to consolidate a relatively unchallenged alliance, the multiplicity of competing social interests prevalent in Argentine society has prevented such an alliance. Agrarian-sector organizations have been consistently more powerful in setting economic priorities and in mobilizing political and social resources to achieve them. Labor organizations achieved institutional and political strength at the same time that private firms became sharply divided between the older industrial firms associated with the UIA and the newer generation of firms associated with the CGE. Foreign firms became important players in the 1960s. Lastly, financial brokers have become an autonomous source of economic power whose goals and objectives can conflict with those of industrial firms.

Second, these patterns of economic conflict have generated peculiar patterns of institutional behavior that have, for the most part, undermined the consolidation of consistent development strategies. Political instability has generated institutional instability, which has meant sudden changes in operational laws and, more generally, constant changes in the rules of the game for social participants. In such a context, organizations tend to try to maximize short-term benefits, and institutional behavior resembles a zero-sum game, if not a negative-sum game. Entrepreneurial organizations, in particular, have given priority to what Alberti and Castiglioni call *movimientista* goals, such as identification, inclusion or exclusion, resource mobilization for opposition purposes, and antagonistic characterization of external forces, over "organizational" goals, such as long-range planning, coordination, interdependency, and interest mediation between external and internal entities (1985).

LABOR

One of the most important characteristics of industrial labor in South Korea has been that, to a large extent, it has been recruited from the countryside. Three and one-half million workers migrated from rural to urban areas in the 1961–1971 period alone (Hsiao 1986:31). In the 1960–1975 period, the working class share of the total labor force grew from 8.7 percent to 21.1 percent, and farmers declined from 66.2 percent to 49.2 percent (Hsiao 1986:34). By 1981, the labor force in industry had grown to 28 percent and declined in agriculture to 34 percent (Barret and Chin 1987:27).

It has often been maintained that the rural background of these workers has led to greater docility and political quiescence. However, this is not clear from South Korea's past. For example, the end of World War II witnessed an impressive phase of labor conflicts. The rapid growth of industry after 1935 was important because it generated a rapid growth in employment (Hamilton 1986:17), creating favorable conditions for the rapid growth of trade unions in the mid-1940s. From this perspective, "The social and regional conflicts that racked Korea in the 1945–53 period have their origins in the immense population shifts, agrarian disruptions, and industrial dynamism of the final phase of the Japanese imperium" (Cummings 1987:57). The end of World War II brought about a fast growth of trade unions. From November to December 1945, trade union membership rose from 200,000 to 533,408 (Choi 1985:8) and culminated in the general strike of 1946 (Hamilton 1986:21). The labor movement underwent a demobilization phase during 1946, when a conservative leadership was used to displace the left. By September 1947, union membership had drastically declined (Choi 1985:8). An important cause of this was the decline in manufacturing following World War II (Kim and Roemer 1979:26–27).

The state response to labor mobilizations in the mid-1940s highlighted the use of repression for years to come. Thus, during the 1950s, ISI "did not have the political characteristics it had in Brazil and elsewhere. Politics did not stretch to include workers, peasants, or plural competition for power" (Cummings 1987:70).

In part, state control of the labor force was made all the more important due to the absence of established control practices within manufacturing firms (such as the use of permanent employment policies). As in Singapore, labor control was exercised by the state, and in an increasingly harsher manner since the early 1970s (Deyo 1987: 183, 195). State involvement has also had a considerable impact on the development of labor organizations. "Until the mid-1970s the national industrial unions that made up the (FKTU) functioned mainly to moderate union demands, implement government policy, and discipline recalcitrant locals" (Deyo 1987:185). In Free Export Zones, the government prohibited strikes and union organization altogether (Cummings 1987:75).

However, this does not mean that workers in South Korea fit the traditional image of extremely low wages. "Real wages in manufacturing remained fairly constant over the decade from 1957 to 1966, but then began a steady rise and more than doubled from 1966 to 1975" (Kim and Roemer 1979:72). Since the mid-1970s, wages for skilled workers was rising at a considerably faster pace than wages for unskilled workers (Kim and Roemer 1979:167). Wage differentials imply a growing militancy among skilled workers. There is evidence of a shortage of skilled labor in the late 1970s, when the migration of construction teams to the Middle East exerted an upward pressure on wages (Cummings 1987:79).

Eighty percent of the workers in the Free Trade Zones is composed of females, primarily teenage women from peasant families (Cummings 1987:74). They are likely to quiesce while they view their wage employment as temporary, but as the social structure becomes more crystallized, possibilities for industrial conflict also arise. Also, a shortage of blue-collar workers influenced labor activism of second-generation industrial workers during the 1970s (Hsiao 1986:40).

The first wave of recent labor conflicts came in the late 1970s, when the strikes and labor mobilizations were frequently organized by independent, grassroots unions (Koo 1987:178). This wave of labor organization was met with repression (Cummings 1987:79). There was also an organizational drive of the FKTU in 1975–1979, followed by a crackdown after 1979 (Deyo 1987:189).

Although these tendencies have led to recent labor instability, pressures are not equally distributed among all manufacturing firms. For example, the rise of wages has gradually undermined competitiveness in the light, labor-intensive manufactures that initially led growth (Haggard and Cheng 1987:86). This is because higher wages in other sectors, such as electronics, are luring workers away from industries, such as textiles, and eventually exert an upward pressure on wages (*Far Eastern Economic Review*, February 26, 1987:48). More recently, business leaders have forecast that rising wages in these industries may lead to loss of jobs to countries such as China and Bangladesh (*The New York Times*, July 11, 1987).

In Argentina, there is a long history of trade unions since the turn of the century. Beginning in the late nineteenth century, the bargaining power of organized labor in Argentina was strengthened by a pervasive shortage of labor. Trade unions grew rapidly during the 1930s, when Communists were successful in organizing industrial unions among workers in construction, meat packing, and textiles. Their strength and ability to mobilize workers in large industrial conflicts was a major factor shaping the emergence of Peronism.

Labor policies after the 1943 coup were designed to challenge the growing predominance of Communist trade unions. As Secretary of Labor, Peron sought trade union support by pushing for higher real wages and encouraging organized labor in their membership drives. Eventually, organized labor became a major component in the political alliance led by the Peron regimes in the 1940s and 1950s. As opposed to similar regimes in Mexico and Brazil, organized labor in Argentina had a greater degree of autonomous power, which they have subsequently sustained for much of the postwar period.

As indicated in the last section, the strong bargaining power of trade unions in the postwar period was made compatible with industrialization through import substitution by means of protectionist structures and an orientation of manufacturing for the domestic market. What was salient about organized labor in Argentina during the 1960s and 1970s was that the expansion of firms producing consumer durables led to an explosion of labor conflicts in the late 1960s. State policies were subsequently unable to check an escalation of strikes during the 1970s.

CONCLUSION

In contrasting Latin American and East Asian countries and strategies for development, the emphasis should not be placed as much on the policies themselves, or in the general orientation of the economy (i.e., import-substituting versus export-oriented). Instead, it seems more enlightening to focus at the level of social institutions and social actors in order to understand the general conditions that guide or underlie development strategies.

In South Korea, the ability of the state and the *chaebol* to maintain a coherent set of objectives and stable mechanisms to achieve them was enhanced by the lack of competing social pressures at the level of institutional political action. Landowners and organized labor were demobilized as a political force in the immediate postwar period. Multinational corporations and financial speculators were successfully screened and regulated by a relatively strong state and did not challenge the basic alliance of state and *chaebol*.

In Argentina, social conflict prevented the adoption of an effective development strategy after the early 1950s. The state never achieved an institutional and organizational coherence that would allow it to function as a broker. In turn, political conflicts had an impact upon the economic terrain. What clearly sets the case of Argentina apart from South Korea was the lack of coherence and continuity in both political legitimacy and economic policy. Within the period of vertical import substitution (1958–1972), there were at least three clearly different subperiods, with divergent economic objectives and policies, implemented by six presidents and a score of economic ministers amongst five military coups. In Argentina, social and political factors played a more prominent role in undermining the vertical import-substitution coalition and in setting the stage for a new set of development patterns.

The timing involved in the development and maturity of the institutional arrangements in both countries suggests that semiperipheral development involves the simultaneous creation of social and institutional constraints to further development. From the standpoint of the sequence of development trajectories, the evidence shows that alliances and coalitions that have been effective at a certain point in time may be undermined by its success at a later point in time. The relationship between the agrarian sector and the state in Argentina between the 1880s and 1930s was as coherent and as effective as the alliance between the state and private industrial capital in South Korea in the 1960s and 1970s. With a clearly defined goal of gaining and maintaining access to the world system through exports of primary products, the alliance of elite sectors in Argentina was successful in maintaining growth policies. This model of external insertion became exhausted after the great depression, but the emergence of competing interests and competing goals, and their conflicting impacts on state structures, undermined the capacity to establish equally efficient alternative models.

With this analytical framework in mind, the recent economic and political transformations in South Korea can be interpreted as a transition toward a more complex set of institutional arrangements, a transition that is emerging out of the very success of rapid capitalist growth. The institutional implications of rapid growth, in other words, are posing an increasingly acute challenge to the peculiar and unique set of social, economic, and institutional arrangements that were highly favorable to economic development in South Korea for the past two decades.

The institutional implications of these transformations can be discerned at four different levels: international economic relations, sectorial cleavages, industrial restructuring, and corporate reorganization. In 1986, Korean exports to the United States grew by 26.2 percent compared to the previous year, making the Korean economy more dependent on U.S. markets, and, thus, more vulnerable to U.S. government demands for greater liberalization of financial, imports, and direct foreign investment markets. The situation is compounded by an increasing Korean dependence on imports from Japan, which, in 1986, comprised 34.4 percent of all South Korean imports, compared to 24.2 percent in 1985. And although the yen has been over valued with respect to the dollar, a delegation of Korean businessmen visiting U.S. industries found very few items that could be profitable exported to Korea. In April 1987, the South Korean government announced a sweeping program of trade liberalization measures (*Asian Wall Street Journal*, March 16, 1987; March 26, 1987; April 27, 1987).

The implementation of liberalization measures has created important cleavages between the executive agencies, such as the Economic

Planning Board, the bureaucratic agencies in charge of implementing policies, and also between smaller and larger firms who are affected differentially by market liberalization (*Asian Wall Street Journal,* March 16, 1987; July 6, 1987). Most importantly, labor unrest and labor demands have been growing through 1987, and they are projected to increase as independent labor organizations consolidate. In fact, the emergence of a strong labor movement may be the most influential event in South Korea in the next few years (*The New York Times,* July 19, 1987).

The rise of the yen and the decline in the value of the dollar in relation to the won, along with the obsolescence of infrastructure and the pressure of foreign competition, have been threatening the survival of firms in traditional export sectors in Korea, such as textiles. The competitiveness of the Korean textile industry has been further undermined by conflicts between small garment producers, corporate garment producers, and yarn producers. The structural problems affecting textile producers are "typical throughout South Korean industry, which tends to be top-heavy, with strong abilities in mass production of fairly uniform products where speedy delivery, rather than original design or innovation, is the most important selling point" (*Far Eastern Economic Review,* February 26, 1987).

The major Korean *chaebol,* which we identified as an important source of economic and institutional power in South Korea, have recently undergone crucial organizational transformations that have gradually replaced personal and political styles of leadership with more strategic and rational ones. This flexibility, along with greater democratization, may help Korea sustain high levels of growth in the current decade.

CHAPTER 7

Export-Oriented Industrialization and Political and Class Development: Hong Kong on the Eve of 1997

B. Karin Chai

Hong Kong's colonial system has fused government with the state, making it an administrative entity without political parties where the highly centralized colonial bureaucracy is accountable to no one and determines and executes politics. Since Hong Kong was established as a result of the Opium War, merchants, bankers, and capitalists were given political influence from early on. And since the traditional elite provides a channel by which the bureaucracy can secure cooperation and legitimacy, this elite was co-opted; that is, it was informally consulted and given a largely ceremonial status. Thus, the decision-making power of the civil service had successfully been united with the wealth of large entrepreneurs and the land-based wealth and status of the traditional elite.

The co-opted merchants, bankers, and industrialists supported the government and its policies, and the government steered clear of policies that might interfere with the economy or have a negative impact on the entrenched interests of the elite. In fact, the interests of all parts of the co-opted elite were so closely fused with those of the top civil servants and the Crown that they became one power elite that has acquired a class character since it not only commands all resources but also "dominates the principal sources of information" (Davies 1977:46).

The close alignment of the traditional elite with the colonial power created a gap between the elites and the popular classes and, hence, a crisis of integration. Even though the middle and lower classes were, theoretically, represented in an ascribed top-down manner, such representation was, at best, haphazard and distorted, for the elite-mass gap did not foster a familiarity with the problems and concerns of the middle and working classes on the part of appointees. Instead, appointments to the Legislative Council, Hong Kong's substitute of a parliament, was primarily based on the appointee's perceived willingness and ability to cooperate with the government.

Government policy subscribed to the laissez-faire ideal and was largely composed of ex-post facto reactions to events or guided by prioritized administrative convenience and the maintenance of public order (Wong 1980). Social policies were confined to providing the minimum and did not apply qualitative standards (Chow 1985a). The Legislative Council remained extremely conservative; the economic elite even stalled attempts by the British labor government for better labor legislation and political reforms, plans for which were floated as early as 1948–1949.

The few attempts by government to improve the situation of the working class fizzled out or were shelved because the colonial government could not afford to alienate its powerful ally. Therefore, no political development occurred, and since the overwhelming part of the population were refugees from Communist rule, they lacked integration and political clout. But the anachronistic colonial system also remained because of the persistence of traditional Chinese political culture, which inclines people to support autocratic, expert-controlled and benevolent government, and to remain politically apathetic.

EXPORT-ORIENTED DEVELOPMENT, THE STRUCTURE OF INDUSTRY, AND THE PETITE BOURGEOISIE

Industrialization by way of export-oriented light industries has been the main vehicle of economic development, which had a 6.4 percent growth rate of real per capita GDP from 1959 to 1976. Manufacturing still contributed 21.7 percent to GDP in 1987 (Hong Kong 1989 Annual Statistics, Table 7.8) and remains an important contributor to the GDP and the third largest sector in terms of employment. Since the economy has not been interfered with by the Hong Kong government and the industries are very dependent on exports (between 80 and 90 percent), manufacturing can serve as an indicator of the class situation resulting from export-oriented development. This chapter analyzes the structure of industry, using organization size as a criterion, to prove the situation of the petite bourgeoisie and of the working class.

Table 7.1

Structure of Industries in Terms of Employment and Size of Industrial Establishments 1961, 1977 and 1986 (in percentages)

	1961	1977	1986
Manufacturing Employment			
Small	84.8	92.1	92.3
Medium	14.3	7.5	7.4
Large	0.9	0.4	0.3
Size Distribution of Manufacturing Establishments			
Small	29.6	40.2	41.1
Medium	47.4	43.1	44.0
Large	23.0	6.7	14.9

Sources: Youngson, A. J., 1982, *Hong Kong: Economic Growth and Policy*, New York: Oxford; *Hong Kong Annual Digest of Statistics*, 1988, Census & Statistics Department, Hong Kong, Table 4.3.

In contrast to Singapore and Korea, virtually all industrial enterprises in Hong Kong have been started with the entrepreneur's own capital. In cases where the planning, design, and marketing are done elsewhere, entrance barriers to industry still remain low and encourage the proliferation of small, narrowly specialized enterprises. Thus, manufacturing enterprises doing simple processing and assembling and employing fewer than twenty workers constitute the majority in Hong Kong, as is the case also in Taiwan. Such industrialization, provided it hits a growth period in the world system, allows a vertical take-off and a fast pace of industrialization since it does not need much capital accumulation. It facilitates the maximal mobilization and utilization of all available manpower, skill, and technology and avoids the pitfalls of a dual economy, since even the smallest enterprises are directly or indirectly integrated into the world market through the subcontracting system. For a summary of such data, see Table 7.1.

However, the combination of a narrow base of financial and managerial resources with a high degree of specialization and exposure to the world market tends to inhibit capital accumulation. Moreover, the division of labor between rather than within enterprises is facilitated through a tight system of subcontracting between firms. Thus, the share of very small manufacturing establishments has increased rather than declined with development, in spite of the fact that they have lower labor productivity and a lower index of census value-added per unit labor cost across various industrial sectors. Their survival and even greater share is generally attributed to their perceived relative efficiency and productivity and especially to their capacity to rapidly adjust to changed market conditions.

The size of organizations reflects qualitative differences in the reproduction of economic classes. Small entrepreneurs are "socially conventional people" and tend to come from families with little "cultural capital" (Sit and Wong 1989:89). Many of them seem to have started their career by chance or as a result of conflict with their partners or shareholders. But they tend to be better educated than petty entrepreneurs and have some command of English. But since most of them are graduates of Chinese schools, they lack the right kind of credentials for entry into stable white-collar jobs. It is the "incompatibility between their relatively high educational attainment and the local opportunity structure that drives them into entrepreneurial activities" (Sit and Wong 1989:6) and to rank themselves in the middle class. These entrepreneurs, together with self-employed craftsmen, hawkers, and small shopkeepers, make up the petite bourgeoisie, which seems to be a highly differentiated and transient class since its members usually expect their children to achieve white-collar status.

Medium entrepreneurs, in contrast, share the market situation of the bourgeoisie together with self-employed professionals, larger shopkeepers, and merchants. Recruitment to this class seems to derive partly from positive factors, such as opportunity structure, the need for autonomy, and the availability of family resources, and partly from negative selection (e.g., lack of competitiveness for stable white-collar employment). Sit and Wong confirm that medium entrepreneurs are likely to come from a higher stratum; that is, they are from families with more cultural capital, start working life as administrators or managers, use more English, have gone to Anglo-Chinese schools, tend to be more profit-oriented, and have higher status aspirations (1989:102–131).

THE SEGMENTATION OF LABOR MARKETS AND THE SITUATION OF THE WORKING CLASS

The lack of working class consciousness is often explained by the fact that female workers and immigrants make up a large share of the industrial work force and that the former especially often are so alienated that they rationalize discrimination rather than protest

(Ng et al. 1987). Only medium- and large-scale enterprises with stable profits offer better benefits and perhaps employment security to retain their staff. Small-scale establishments balance the changing impact of the world market, passed on through the subcontracting network, by adjusting their establishment size and stratifying their internal labor market.

Deyo, in that volume, sees labor market shelters as alternate systems of labor expropriation or subsistence strategies and argues that each system relies on a unique pattern of labor expropriation. The sheltering of workers thus defines an institutional boundary between market and nonmarket labor systems, rather than between divergent markets. The patterns of labor expropriation most relevant for Hong Kong industry are patriarchy and bureaucratic paternalism. The first prevails in small enterprises, where kinship rights and obligations govern relations of production and where "controls are informal and extensive," but where the patriarchal authority itself is tightly regulated by norms of noneconomic reciprocity and mutual obligation.

Both labor market types, patriarchy and bureaucratic paternalism, are efficient in absorbing conflict, preventing the development of class consciousness, and leading at best to "kitchen" or "office" politics, (e.g., the neutralization or diffusion of social constraints and the personalization of problems). Both help to maintain industrial peace in spite of exploitation of labor in export-led development which, at times, even substitutes labor for capital.

Both market types are anchored in the same norms which reinforce authoritarianism of employers and conformity and submission of employees. The traditional prejudice against manual work, reinforced by poor working conditions, relatively low pay compared to other sectors, and the absence of career prospects and often also of employment security, put workers in their place and kept them occupied with everyday concerns. Neither the labor market nor traditional culture encouraged them to develop aspirations other than those which could be achieved by way of hard work and supported by a belief that "Hong Kong is a land of abundant opportunity" (Lau and Kuan 1988:6).

Employment in larger industrial establishments, especially in textiles and electronics, closely resembles paternal bureaucratism except that it differs in the general absence of promotion opportunities and career ladders. In the other sectors of the economy, the segmentation of the labor market is reinforced by the public and semipublic (utilities) sectors topping off the status hierarchy. But the structural separation of labor markets does not facilitate consciousness or attempt to overcome the fragmented class situation of the petite bourgeoisie either.

As consumers, the working class is highly dependent on, and has developed a strong output orientation towards, the government for the provision of services. Its members feel that government should take care of their needs, especially since employers often fail to do so (Turner 1980:176ff.). They expect the government to put pressure on employers to make them fulfill their contractual obligations. Thus, the political interests of the working class are largely confined to restitution of injustice, to legislation or implementation that safeguard their interests, or to bread-and-butter issues related to basic needs such as housing, safety, sanitation, transport, and education.

CAPITALIST DEVELOPMENT, EMERGENCE OF THE MIDDLE CLASS, AND THE ROLE OF PROFESSIONALS

The development of industries brought a higher standard of living, the expansion of all kinds of services, and the rapid growth of the public sector with government spending on social services increasing sixfold from 2.662 billion HK$ in 1973 to 19.112 billion HK$ in 1984. However, this growth only reflects the sixfold increase in GDP in the same period, and the average annual increase in public expenditure of 19.4 percent was only slightly higher than the 18.2 percent average growth rate of the GDP (Chow 1985a:477). However, the massive and sustained growth of the economy, helped by a decline of the population growth rate, resulted in the creation of a middle class which was helped by the provision of low-cost housing and expansion of education.

The rapid expansion of services especially improved the market position of professionals such as medical doctors, lawyers, accountants, or social workers. Since they enjoyed a relatively high prestige, they also were able to partly fill the niche that was opening through the declining influence of the traditional elite, which had lost its resource basis (land) through the development of the new towns, and which, as a class, had failed to upgrade its educational level. Professionals in civil service are a modern version of the gentry and form the apex of the status hierarchy. Moreover, the cultural fragmentation of the survival-oriented refugee of the 1950s and 1960s slowly shifted to a common Hong Kong culture-based on the Cantonese dialect and common identity as Hong Kong citizens. Since professionals have the means to choose their style of life and exert considerable influence on public opinion, they became the carriers of the Hong Kong culture and the aspirations of the wider middle class, especially the lower white-collar workers.

But professionals in bureaucratic employment experience a strong dose of employer-employee conflict because of their claim to professional autonomy, their widespread discrimination vis-à-vis expatriates in terms of pay and benefits in the civil service, and because of the reforms of the civil service since 1972. Consequently, professional associations mushroomed and began to protest and take industrial action against their employers, mainly the government. The not fully-autonomous professions shared, to some extent in this conflict, but their concerns also were partly directed against the barriers to mobility established by the full professions. Their protests often constituted usurping action, like the fight of the nurses against the authority of medical doctors in hospitals. Thus, the extensive unionization in the white-collar sector starting in the 1970s resulted from status rather than class competition (Semyonov and Lewin-Epstein 1989:390).

Nonetheless, white-collar unionism had a number of important effects. It helped to institutionalize Western-style adversarial labor-management relations in Hong Kong, fostered a belief in self-help, provided a model for blue-collar unions, and proved a valuable organizational experience which could be applied in the fight for greater political participation.

ECONOMIC DEVELOPMENT AND ITS IMPACT

From the 1970s, Hong Kong's economy edged towards that of a typical industrialized nation. Individual industries diversified and upgraded many of their operations. For example, the share in employment of the textile industry as percentage of total employment in manufacturing declined from 32 percent in 1950 to 14 percent in 1980, while the more capital- and skill-intensive clothing industry increased its share in the same period from 3 to 29 percent. Such upgrading of industries was not simply an adjustment in the manufacturing cycle but constituted "a shift of resources" (Scott 1989:234) resulting in drastic movements upward of the occupational structure. Manufacturing declined, commerce increased, and services shifted from the underdeveloped unskilled type to sophisticated business, financial, and community services. The expansion of the public sector contributed to the growth of services as did the development of banking due to changes in banking laws. Money flowed into Hong Kong, which became a regional financial center. In 1986, the financial sector alone employed over 6 percent of the work force, and, as Table 7.2 shows, it contributed more to GDP than industries.

The diversification and development of the economy had considerable repercussions on Hong Kong's standing in the world economy, on the role of government, on the market situation of different classes, and on class relations. The economic development helped Hong Kong to maintain and expand its international stature as a

Table 7.2
Share in Employment and Contribution to GDP of the Economic Sectors, HK 1961–1986
(in percentages)

	1961	1971	1980	1986
Agriculture, Mining, Fishing	8	4	1	0.2
Manufacturing Industry	42	49	42	35.9
Construction	4	6	8	6.3
Utilities	2	1	0.5	6.6
Commerce	12	13	25	28.8
Transport and Telecommunications	8	7	7.5	8
Services	24	20	16	18.1
Total Number	1,130,700	1,557,000	2,268,900	2,744,818

Source: Youngson, A. J., 1982, *Hong Kong: Economic Growth and Policy*, p. 17, New York: Oxford.

port and to become a major stock market and regional financial center. Due to the declining growth rate of the world economy in the 1970s and 1980s, the growing trend towards protectionism and the "second wave" of Asian industrialization, Hong Kong industries were under pressure to upgrade. They started to take on a role in technology transfer from the center to the periphery by opening production plants in other Southeast Asian countries or by adapting technology from the center to the more labor-intensive needs of Third World countries (Lall 1984).

As a result, Hong Kong's place in the world system moved from the periphery to the semiperiphery. Hong Kong became more tightly and more complexly integrated into the world economy, which, in turn, fostered a more outward-looking orientation to markets, other regions, and the center. The upgrading of skills allowed a greater transferability of skills and higher mobility of the Hong Kong population in and out of Hong Kong society. But the slower growth of the world economy also narrowed the ecological niche for Hong Kong's manufacturing industries and made them more fragile, thereby reinforcing the tendency towards an expansion of the service sector and internationalization.

Economic development also tended to expand the role of government. The government's role was always important because it was the largest employer and provider of welfare services. But in line with changes in the economy, government changed from one that (incorrectly) claimed to adhere to "laissez faire" to one that practiced "positive noninterventionism." The labels reflect government's reluctance to admit its greater role. But it had become more important in planning for the operation and expansion of the economy through the provision of a more capital-intensive infrastructure and the negotiation of access to markets. It also had to regulate the market, for example, by providing guidelines for the operation of banks and stock markets, and sometimes, it even had to make up for failures of the market mechanism. Capitalist development drives towards big government since an advanced complex economy needs international integration and coordination, predictability of various high-quality services, a framework for the operation of market forces, and control of its excesses. These pressures drove the government to the expansion of services, more planning, and a higher level of involvement, which altogether gave it a dominant influence in and on the economy.

ENTREPOT TRADE AND THE ECONOMIC ROLE OF CHINA

China provided not only the impetus but also the skill and much of the money for Hong Kong's industrialization. While this happened accidentally, Hong Kong's entrepot trade with China provided an important, if varying, sector of economic activity. But Hong Kong's population depended on imports of agricultural and cheap consumer goods to such an extent that China is more aptly described as a silent partner in the Hong Kong enterprise. China's economic reforms and its opening in 1978 broadened its role and strengthened its weight in Hong Kong. The mainland became a dominant player on the Hong Kong market, both commercially and financially, in manufacturing and in banking. The volume and nature of trade between Hong Kong and China changed, and the regional integration between Guangdong and Hong Kong (and Macao) got well under way with considerable repercussions not only on the Pearl River Delta but also on Hong Kong's economy.

China expanded its economic foothold in the colony by a variety of strategic investments and is now the third largest investor in manufacturing in Hong Kong (Scott 1989:226). China controls the second largest group of banks, giving it a hold on the property market, and it has established a number of trading companies in the territory. That China not only has a foothold in the economy but also is pursuing an active policy is demonstrated by its financial transactions, which have changed from a surplus of nearly 5,000 HK$ in early 1979 to a deficit of 13,708 HK$ at the end of June 1984 (Jao 1985:369). It is thought that as many as 30,000 mainland Chinese are, more or less, permanently stationed in Hong Kong.

The opening of China was a windfall for Hong Kong's manufacturing industries, which had been in dire straits because the severe labor shortage, combined with property speculations, had driven production prices so high that small manufacturing enterprises could only survive by moving up market or by relocating to China. And since China invited foreign investments with the establishments of special economic zones in Shenzhen and Chuhai, Hong Kong entrepreneurs were quick to seize the opportunity. By mid-1989, a total of 8,691 Hong Kong-led enterprises were established in China (SCMP July 6, 1989), and Hong Kong's investments in Guangdong alone had a total contract value of 9.1 billion US$. It is estimated that 90 percent of the production of Hong Kong's garments, toys, electronics, appliances, and giftwares is now done in China.

IMPACT OF CHANGES ON CLASSES

The diversification of industries resulted in the differentiation of the bourgeoisie and fragmentation of interests within and between the strata. It separated the formerly closely allied interests of the financial and business sector from that of industrialists and opened a gulf between those having allied their fortune with China and those having an interest in preserving the international status of the territory. Moreover, company owners are increasingly replaced by technocrats, whose contradictory class position makes them unreliable allies in the pursuit of class interests. To the previously existing local-foreign, big-small divisions there were now added international versus China, services versus industry, and owner versus technocrat divisions, all of which contributed to the failure of the bourgeoisie to develop common civic interests and become an organized political force.

Not all classes have profited equally from development, and it seems that the situation of the workers has not substantially improved or may have relatively worsened. For one, wages tend to rise slower and fall faster than the economy, and fluctuations hit workers hard. While the growth rate of GDP was around 8 percent in the 1950s and 1960s, the 1970s twice (1974 and 1975) saw a decline in per capita GDP (by -3 and -15 percent, respectively), and even though the average rate of growth for per capita GDP for the decade from 1973 to 1982 was 6.3 percent, it fluctuated wildly from, for example, 10.1 percent in 1973 to -0.3 percent in 1974 (Scott 1989:129).

A tight market or profit situation also makes employers resort to a temporary or shifting labor force, resulting in declining opportunities for overtime pay (a very important part of the average worker's pay package) and less employment security. Often, employers evade even their minimal legal obligations to workers, which is still the most common cause of industrial disputes in spite of or because of advanced development (Turner 1980:100). Since Hong Kong industrialists employ directly or indirectly a much larger work force in China as in Hong Kong (1.5 million versus 180,000), employment in Hong Kong's industries has been drastically affected. It also has potentially opened the door for a greater influx of legal and illegal workers, who undermine wage levels (Ng and Sit 1990:209) and tend to intensify the competition at the periphery. They constitute a potential lumpen proletariat as long as they are not fully integrated into Hong Kong society.

Thus, the working class has also become more highly differentiated. It consists of a relatively permanent, but small substratum of not fully-integrated immigrants from China or, recently, from Vietnam who work occasionally, often as unpaid family workers, as general laborers in construction, or in what is known as tolerated illegal industrial enterprises. Above them is the relatively large stratum of semiskilled operatives (often females) and a smaller stratum of skilled workers who virtually command an internal labor market monopoly. People like hawkers and other self-employed nonprofessional workers may be added depending on the amount of income they secure.

Until very recently, blue-collar unions either understood themselves as patriarchal family enterprises, as recreational clubs, or as subservient handmaidens to the party (the CCP or the GMD). In any case, they lacked recognition by employers and were unable to fight for the rights of workers (Chai 1990). The working class had looked to the government for help. However, the latter has been singularly unresponsive to the needs of the workers since it is closely allied with the entrenched elite. Even when the working class joined with the professional middle class and agitated for a compulsory retirement fund, they failed. Bearing the crunch of the structural changes and faced with the triple failure of employers, unions, and government to be responsive to their needs, working class frustrations can easily lead to anomie, violence, or political crisis.

POLITICAL INSTITUTIONS AND PATTERNS OF REFORM

In spite of Hong Kong's good record for stability, there were periods of unrest in 1956, 1967, and 1968, of which only the last incidence was a spillover from the Cultural Revolution in China. The former were escalated industrial disputes with political overtones. The 1956 crisis was instigated by Taiwan-affiliated unions; the 1967 one was led by Communist-affiliated unions. Both resulted from lack of consensus of the population with the Hong Kong government and were crises of legitimacy (Scott 1988; Leung 1989). Thus, the unrest revealed the fragility of the public order. But it was the 1968 disturbances that confronted the government with widespread discontent which could easily be directed against it, especially since the traditional welfare associations *(kaifongs)* had eroded (Lau 1985). The government was seen as closed, unresponsive, and colonial. It lacked communication with ordinary citizens, and the existence of widespread corruption undermined its legitimacy.

In response to the disturbances, the government attempted to improve public order by soliciting grassroot support and by co-opting a wider part of the population into its consultative network. It established district offices as appendages to the centralized civil service bureaucracy. These were supposed to provide communication channels for the grassroot population and to make the bureaucracy more responsive to local needs. They also were useful for top-down communication and provided instruments of information and control. The district offices also were intended to promote community building by forming and supervising Mutual Aid Committees (MACs), especially in public housing blocks. The government also formed representative advisory area committees which, together with the MACs, helped to integrate wider circles of the population into the advisory network.

These structures were preferred over a more widely advocated ombudsman scheme, for example, because district officers could closely control the advisory bodies and effectively filter upward communication. They were, in short, typical bureaucratic social control devices to accommodate and mute the expression of conflict and helped to absorb and channel the talents of the working class (Katz 1983:115). Scott argues that they did not constitute genuine political reforms but were aimed at "extending administrative penetration to the local level" (Scott 1989:140). Nevertheless, MACs were directed at the working class, and even though they were reigned in tightly or simply dissolved if they became too vocal, they constituted a forum for discussion and created a new, albeit narrow, space for local politics.

Subsequently, under the governorship of MacLehose (1972–1983), the government supplemented such measures by improving the living conditions through decentralization of congested areas, by providing more and better education, housing, and medical services, and by changing to a clean government image. These achievements were possible only with a greatly enlarged public sector, an expanded and improved civil service, and a more forward-looking planning government.

The government's authority increased with its more efficient delivery of services and its forward approach to planning, which promoted citizenship and the identification of Hong Kong people with their society. This greater identification led to the articulation of demands and interests by the professional stratum of the middle class, which had learned from its white-collar union experience and found a political vacuum between government and society. They shared with the working class an interest both in more and better services from the government and, to a much greater extent, in greater political representation. Since the bourgeoisie was divided among itself and had "failed to develop its own aspirations" (Lau 1985:29), the professional stratum found little competition and became the carrier of the movement. Their motivation came from an identification with Hong Kong society and the inconsistency between their high professional autonomy and prestige on the one hand, and their political impotence on the other. The combination of achievement, market position, and social status allowed them to fulfill the elitarian requirements of popular political culture for proper rank and suitability for politics.

The professional stratum formed an alliance with the working class. They started to apply qualitative criteria to the social service delivery and became slightly more critical of the costs of economic growth and the (non)distribution of its benefits. Their proliferating pressure groups took on the role of a watchdog of society, and, through their influence especially on newspapers, they broke the interpretative monopoly of the elite and started to influence public opinion. They introduced new methods of participation: protests, community mobilization, and campaigns which provided an alternative to the informal behind-the-scenes maneuvering of the entrenched elite.

The public discussions in the mass media, meetings, and public seminars led by the professional sector broadened Hong Kongers' concerns from the narrow confines of utilitarian familism typical of the 1960s and early 1970s and laid the foundation for a more critical public attitude. It also helped to undermine some of the authoritarian tendencies of traditional Chinese political culture, (e.g., to accept rather than deny the existence of conflict, and to connect private troubles with public concerns). These changes laid the ground for political expression and undermined the proverbial political apathy of the masses.

The professionals lacked an alternative (or even a common) ideology, and the parochialism of the political culture provided for only a narrow, issue-based legitimacy on condition of a credible claim to representativeness of a wider public. Thus, the liberal pressure groups, made up mostly of younger professionals, were mainly concerned with and confined to bread-and-butter issues such as housing, education, and costs of transportation.

Because of their vocal public methods, their watchdog role, their assertiveness, their alliance with the lower class, and the lack of competition from the petite bourgeoisie, the professional pressure groups became more influential and had to be given some representation in political institutions. This quite suited the civil service which, thereby, could strengthen its hand vis-à-vis the entrenched elite.

Against this were the interests of the bourgeoisie and their fear of the masses, the disdain of the bureaucracy for politicians, and the overall elitist political culture, all of which stultified any impetus toward wider representation. In spite of a move towards localization and the introduction of indirectly elected members to the Legislative Council, the representation of professionals on the Council increased very slowly, and in 1986, they were still outnumbered by business representatives (Davies 1989:36–76, Tables 1, 3, 5). The government tried to appease the middle class and compensate for the lack of representation of professionals, on the one hand, by the provision of more and better social services and, on the other, by developing district boards into an "institutional focus for local political activity" (Scott 1989:144). They allowed the professional middle class to penetrate community politics, but in the process, the latter edged out working class representatives and shifted the focus of the local community away from the Mutual Aid Committees.

THE SINO-BRITISH AGREEMENT AND THE LIMITS OF REFORM

With the approach of 1997, when the rented new territories were to be returned to the People's Republic of China (PRC), pressure was exerted on Britain to negotiate a solution that would maintain the political and economic autonomy of Hong Kong. The Sino-British Agreement (SBA) of 1984, however, restores Hong Kong to the PRC, into which it will be fully integrated by 2047. Starting from 1997, Hong Kong is to be a special administrative region with a high degree of autonomy under the "one country, two systems" formula and can maintain its capitalist system. Both Britain and China have a commitment to a smooth transition and the maintenance of stability and prosperity since destabilization or decline would mean a loss of face for both of them.

In spite of the fact that the people of Hong Kong had not been consulted, the SBA relieved some of the H.K. jitters and was generally accepted on the basis of either nationalist feelings or the perception of a useful role for Hong Kong in China's modernization process (supported by the extremely rapid regional integration between Hong Kong and Guangdong under the impact of reforms). There also was the clear understanding that the Hong Kong government would pursue the political reforms as promised by Britain's government and by the Green Paper "On the Development of Representative Government in Hong Kong," which was released shortly before the signing of the SBA.

Political modernization in Hong Kong was to be much more limited than the Hong Kong government had anticipated. This became obvious through the conflict-laden negotiations on the implementation of the SBA which escalated into megaphone diplomacy and tit-for-tat retributions in the autumn of 1989. The ground swell of frustrations generated by political and economic factors was whipped up by the Beijing massacre, leading many H.K. people to accept a direct conflict with China and to open defiance of the wishes of their future ruler. It had become clear that the iron guarantees of the SBA did not bind China for two reasons. One was that the SBA promised a high degree of autonomy for Hong Kong and did not make specific provisions for how these objectives were to be achieved. "What was wrong with the agreement was not what it said but what it did not say" (Scott 1989:213), for it allowed different interpretations, which, in Hong Kong, were misguided by wishful thinking and, in Britain, by a narrow legalistic interpretation and a total lack of understanding of Chinese politics. Young points out that the "lack of specifics may be explained by Chinese interpretation of capitalism as simply an economic system" (1985:103).

The other reason is that Communist China always interprets every aspect of social, economic, or political reality in the light of the principles of the dictatorship of the proletariat, the supremacy of collective interests, party leadership, mass line, and socialist democracy. Moreover, the traditional Chinese claim to centrality is part and parcel of China's willingness to allow a high degree of autonomy within the special administrative region (Young 1985:102). Chinese dynasties have always attempted "not only to extract resources from the periphery but to permeate it and to reconstruct it symbolically and to mobilize it structurally" (Eisenstadt 1985:27). Therefore, the lack of detail in the SBA was designed to leave enough room for the PRC to define its meanings in small and well-timed doses of information released through carefully selected channels and to finally impose its interpretative perspective upon Hong Kong citizens. Thus, the definition of autonomy, whether nominal or real, the starting time of the transition period, 1997 or 1984, and consequently, the role of Britain and China up to 1997 and the definition of a Chinese citizen and his rights, all have remained at issue. Since China insisted on its own interpretation and on the need for convergence of the pre-1997 and the post-1997 decisions, the British government had to give in step by step, and the Hong Kong government could only "rationalize the decisions on which it had no influence" (Scott 1989). The Tienanmen massacre jolted Hong Kong's people out of their political apathy. It demonstrated very clearly the coercion China is willing to use against its citizens and robbed Hong Kong's people of their belief in the personal integrity of China's leaders, especially Deng Hsiao Peng, whom they had seen as guarantors of the political order and of Hong Kong's future.

COMPETING AUTHORITIES AND THE CRISIS OF LEGITIMATION

The 13-year transition period institutionalizes two competing authorities with different philosophies and methods of operation. This not only creates double standards and grey areas, but also undermines each authority and provides a breeding ground for all sorts of crises, political cynicism, anomie, and instability (Pye 1973). Competing authority means lack of authority, inefficiency, and poor service delivery, which in Hong Kong means political disruption. The SBA negotiations had already shown the impotence of the lame duck Hong Kong government. Not only is the Hong Kong government restricted by the veto power of Beijing, but it is virtually held hostage by its own citizens. The economic elite, as well as many smaller entrepreneurs and businessmen, have made an alliance with Beijing and are holding the government at ransom (Young 1985). The professional middle class, if not opting out, is using the exodus of their colleagues to press for better or quicker pay of their pensions, presumably to be able to buy themselves a foreign passport.

Seeing itself as a sort of shadow government, China needs an organizational basis other than that provided by the quasiconsular New China News Agency. But there is no adequate institutional frame for its participation. Partly for this reason, but also because the formal political system is British, China operates mainly outside the formal political institutions. It is trying to create shadow institutions to limit British influence and to penetrate the grassroots in order to contain destabilizing tendencies. China also aims at alliances with strategic groups such as businessmen, industrialists, traditional associations, and civil servants, and has undertaken a massive drive using all sorts of methods, such as simple persuasion, information dissemination, the establishment of a client relationship, or a united front strategy. All organizations are used—unions, banks, and firms—to establish grassroot support in the upcoming elections; China also has started to build up residents' associations.

The SBA had a different impact on different classes in Hong Kong, on their interrelations and alliances, and on the overall political process. The working class as a whole stands to gain class status even though the value of such status is doubtful. It provides a potential political tool for China, especially in the highly unionized utilities sector, and some workers' organizations recently have become more articulate, putting pressure on the Hong Kong government partly in the established pattern of consumer demands for better services, but partly also for patriotic reasons, such as the protest against Vietnam refugees in September 1989. Since the nationalistic feelings of the working class are deep and it has no possibility to opt out of Hong Kong society, its interests are closely allied with China. Therefore, workers tend to have a longer term political sentiment, with emphasis on gradual change in China rather than in Hong Kong.

For the time being, the feelings of the lower classes are swayed by nationalism, fear of upheaval, frustrated aspirations, and greater economic insecurity, partly reinforced by the import of foreign labor. The transition to 1997 and the creation of a functional constituency for labor have raised the stakes of the political game and made politics more suspect and threatening. Lau and Kuan conclude that "the 1997 malaise simultaneously gives an impetus to political participation, raises political fears, and causes political withdrawal" (1988:81). Survey results of the Hong Kong in Transition to 1997, however, indicate that this is more true for the working class than for the middle class (Hong Kong in Transition to 1997, Research Report). After the protests of 1989, political apathy has increased again. However, if either nationalism declines or the frustrations increase, explosive reactions and insurrection are possible.

The alliance between the working and middle classes is breaking up because their political interests tend to diverge. The middle class concentrates on short-term political changes in Hong Kong; the working class strives for long-term convergence, improvements, and democratization in China. Moreover, the professional middle class, which has been carrying the political movement, is leaving the field through brain drain. The lower class can only align itself with the business class; however, their interests have been driven far apart in the course of the 1970s, and they share little common ground beyond a general desire for stability, prosperity, and consensus.

The professional middle class stands to lose in terms of status and political representation. They face the prospect of integration into the dictatorship of the proletariat and have been most closely allied with the Hong Kong British government. They and their children also are likely to pay the highest opportunity costs. Moreover, having been most closely associated with liberal pressure groups or counter-revolutionary elements, they are likely to face discrimination, for they have failed in their patriotic duty to show loyalty and are, therefore, not even entitled to a claim on human rights unless they mend their ways. As a result, the professional middle class is either making an exit or is capitalizing on this brain drain by exploiting the scarcity of professionals to drive for more or faster pay (presumably to join the exodus). Professionals are more politicized, pushing for democratization before 1997. However, their perspective and time frame differ from that of the working class, and this is bound to drive apart their precarious alliance, which is based on the pursuit of better services.

The business class wants to maximize profits, China wants to maximize stability, and that makes for good bedfellows. Since their wealth buys them life chances anywhere, the economic elite feel no threat from the impending change in sovereignty in 1997. Besides, many of them are "born again" Chinese who have rediscovered their roots in China or simply have investments there. Moreover, they fear instability, over democratization, and political participation by nonelites. They share the "contemptuous and disdainful attitudes" of the civil servants towards "politicians" (Lau 1985). Since they equate democracy with the adoption of redistributive measures and government interference and do not realize that the bigger role of government is a consequence of the development of capitalism itself, they favor a corporatist political system and oppose any impetus for wider representation.

Stratification lines in Hong Kong have always been relatively fluid because of high economic growth, successive waves of immigration, and the easy translation of wealth into prestige and influence. However, with a greater dominance of China in Hong Kong affairs, stratification lines are changing, and classes are competing more with each other, thereby reinforcing crises of authority and tendencies toward anomie. China has already added ethnic and political stratification lines. And the establishment of a client network, together with frozen mobility channels, will likely produce some sort of political brokerage system. The change of sovereignty involves a shift to different forms of social control. This not only affects the process of building institutions, but also raises uncertainty and produces a highly tense political climate which increases the tendencies to instability.

THE CONTRIVING OF REFORM

In order to contain Beijing's influence in the future and to satisfy at least some of the demands proliferating from the uncertainty and the legitimation crisis, the Hong Kong government started to actively contrive reform. But the initial attempt in the 1984 Green Paper "On the Development of Representative Government in Hong Kong," which was the most liberal document yet, has quickly been abandoned because of China's and the economic elite's resistance to them. The diluted changes that were implemented were double-sided, playing the liberal democrats off against the business elite. On the one hand, they were designed to "buy time" for the business elite which had been unprepared for the election game at the earlier stage (Lau 1985); on the other hand, they were to satisfy the demands of the liberals. Consequently, the new Legislative Council had a larger elected element but also an overrepresentation of business people.

The introduction of functional constituencies set interest groups against each other, deepening narrow political fractions and reinforcing parochial politics. Moreover, the preemptory designation of functional constituencies arbitrarily ruled some interests as legitimate and left others out. This came after the stakes in the political game had been raised, and it deepened the resentment of groups that felt cheated. On the whole, the corporatist policies polarized politicians into opposite camps. The penetration of the liberal elements of the middle class into the Legislative Council further underlined the existence of a legitimacy crisis by demonstrating the lack of agreement about the legitimate nature of authority and the proper responsibilities of government. Moreover, the heated discussions of the political model and the shape of elections bypassed the lower classes and lost their support. This demonstrated the existence of a participation crisis (Pye 1973:50–51).

In conclusion, the political process has failed to expand the capacities of political institutions for several reasons: it sought to displace rather than respond to popular aspirations; it was only half-hearted; and it was adopted by a government which had already lost its claim to authority by its failure to live up to the needs of the people. Thus, the political process toward democratization in Hong Kong is a purely transitional phenomenon. It is based on a political alliance of the liberal professionals and working class with the following consequences:

1. Since the working class is mainly interested in concerns of its livelihood and the liberals mainly in democratization, the focus of the political

process oscillates between the two. Moreover, since there are no political parties, mobilizing occurs through a network of friends and clients, which very quickly uses up prestige and, therefore, does not sustain political momentum. Similarly, the alignments of groups is shifting and is driven by events because mobilization is based on a narrow parochial ideology and effected through personal networks.

2. The interests of the middle class and the working class are separating. The view of the middle class is short-term, political, and focused on Hong Kong. That of the working class focuses on long-term changes in China, stability, and convergence of pre- and post-1997 processes. Therefore, the political interests of the lower class and that of the bourgeoisie and economic elite are identical, but their divergent economic interests, along with the pattern of the past, are likely to keep them from making an alliance.

3. The government and middle class have charged the political process with a mission, thereby discrediting politics and increasing fears of instability, reinforcing authoritarian tendencies, especially among capitalists and the working class.

4. The level of awareness of the Hong Kong people has increased, but their willingness to express their interests through regular political channels has decreased because the elites, the government, and the SBA failed to adequately advance a political process of inclusion. Strikes could, therefore, change in nature from simple protests aiming at restitution of contractual relations and take on an emotional and insurrectionist character.

5. Since China as the future ruler has a legitimate interest in Hong Kong politics but no institutionalized role to play, it has created alternative political institutions, subverting the formal political system and reinforcing the legitimation crisis.

6. The institutionalization of competing authorities undermines both of them, leading to anomie, grey areas, inefficiencies, crises, and changing stratifications. Together with the impacts of structural changes of the economy, this provides for political instability, a tendency which is increasing the longer the transition lasts and the more the two authorities are competing.

7. The "one country, two systems" formula cannot work in the way it is generally expected. Since China insists on the full transfer of sovereignty and imposes its own political perspective, it will dominate Hong Kong politics and abort the pre-1997 political process.

8. The tendencies toward instability and crises resulting from the transition will increase the brain drain, especially from the professional middle class. Therefore, additional qualified people will likely be imported from China. This will be stabilizing politically but will decrease the economic competitiveness of Hong Kong and reduce the efficiency of its public services.

9. Given the general elitist, conservative, and patriarchal political ethos, there is no alternative ideology to motivate and legitimate change besides narrow sectional interests, and the rewards for politics are, therefore, minimal. Moreover, since even the Communists are capitalists, the ideological quagmire reinforces ambivalence. Thus, politics in Hong Kong divides people more than it integrates them.

10. The Hong Kong government will have to actively cooperate with the Chinese government to find a way to stop the blackmail of the professional middle class and business. Failing any successful measure and given the highly emotional political climate, China may find itself forced to adopt much stronger methods, like mobilizing the unions in a general strike, bringing down the Hong Kong government to arrest the destabilizing tendencies, and imposing its own authoritarian regime.

CHAPTER 8

Thailand and the World:
The Transformation to Modernity

Eliezer B. Ayal

Over the last three decades, Thailand has been undergoing a major, albeit mostly silent, revolution. This is reflected in almost every aspect of life inside the country and its relations with the rest of the world.

BACKGROUND: SOME UNIQUE FEATURES

Some of these changes parallel similar developments in a number of other Third World countries, but there are situations and changes that are specific to Thailand. The question of the uniqueness of Thailand has been occupying Thailand scholars for decades. The major factor giving rise to the claim of uniqueness is the fact that of all the countries in South and Southeast Asia, only Thailand was never a colony. The implications of this go beyond national pride. For our purposes here, it primarily meant that the exposure of the Thai people to Western civilization was very limited and controlled. The government acted as a filter deciding what, how much, and in what form the foreign ideas were allowed to reach the population. This, combined with the nature of the Thai-Buddhist culture, the interests of the Thai elite, and the caution against giving the surrounding colonialists an excuse to attack Thailand, resulted in a very slow pace of modernization and development until the middle of the twentieth century.

The above does not exhaust the implications and the legacy of the uniqueness which continues to influence events in Thailand even as it develops. An obvious and easily demonstrable example is the extreme primacy of its urban population. Bangkok's population is more than thirty times larger than the population of the next largest city. This cannot be found in any other country at a similar level of per capita income or, for that matter, at any level of per capita income. Almost all of the very substantial industrialization during the last three decades (especially the first two) has taken place in Bangkok and its surroundings. The percentage of the population that lives in rural areas is still around 80 percent, which, again, is the highest of any country with similar per capita income.

Thailand also has a king who wields substantial power and influence in spite of his being, officially, only a constitutional monarch. He has been a major contributor to political stability in a country where political parties in the Western sense are only now emerging. It is difficult to recall any other country, including Japan, with a similar arrangement.

Another special feature of Thailand, which is very much linked to its recent economic success, is the way it has handled the Chinese minority. In brief, Thailand currently is in the process of transforming its Chinese residents into Thais. Since the overwhelming majority of businessmen in Thailand are Chinese or people of Chinese origin, this policy has caught two birds with one stone. It removed the restrictions on the Chinese businessmen, a move which has substantially contributed to the country's development. At the same time, it weakened the remaining taboos among indigenous Thais against engaging in business. In other words, being a true Thai no longer excludes being a businessman.

This important change in policy introduced in the late 1950s and early 1960s was part of a general change in attitude toward business, including foreign investment. The change has also involved new fiscal and monetary policies which have increasingly become much more vigorous and daring, a marked departure from the traditionally cautious policies of the past (Ayal 1961; 1962).

NEW EXTERNAL INFLUENCES AND ASSOCIATIONS

Much of the inspiration for such changes came from the World Bank and the missions it periodically sent to Thailand. The fact that such missions were encouraged to come was in itself an important symptom of the opening up of Thailand and its increasing involvement with the international community. A significant aspect of its foreign involvement was Thailand's agreement, albeit under substantial pressure from the United States, to be a founding member of SEATO; to send troops to the Korean War; as well as to provide help to the United States in its Vietnam operations, including permission for American bombers to use air bases in Thailand for missions over Vietnam and Cambodia. Such one-sided commitment is not typical Thai behavior and was largely inspired by the need to have a protector against the perceived danger from Communist China and the traditionally aggressive Vietnamese, whose espousal of Communism made them even more menacing.

In spite of the fact that these and similar dangers have not entirely disappeared, the important changes and configurations in the world in general, and in Southeast Asia in particular, have ushered in very significant changes in Thailand's policies. Although one should avoid the temptation of putting an exclusive emphasis on a single event as a watershed, some events are clear signposts of change. President Nixon's trip to Communist China in 1972 was such a signpost. This visit shocked Thailand on various levels, not the least of which was the fact that Thailand was not consulted or even informed about the various secret negotiations leading to this momentous change in U.S. policy toward China.

China always loomed large in Thailand's foreign policy. Besides its huge size, geographic proximity, and historical interactions (Thailand used to send tribute missions to China in earlier periods), China was the country of origin of a significant number of Thailand's residents. After Sun Yat Sen established a republican government in China, the Chinese residents in Thailand began to demonstrate Chinese nationalistic feelings and organizations which caused great apprehension among the Thais. This was an important reason why the Thai authorities proceeded with policies designed to control the activities of its Chinese residents (Ayal 1969). On the foreign policy level, the Thai people created difficulties for the Chinese government and its embassy in Bangkok to establish contacts with and influence upon the resident Chinese. When the Communists took over the government in China in 1949, Thailand did not recognize the new government and continued to maintain its diplomatic relations with the very much weakened Republic of China in Taiwan. Since such policy paralleled that of the United States until the Nixon trip, this communality of interest provided an important dimension to Thai-U.S. relations which was later shattered by that trip.

The termination of the unsuccessful U.S. effort in Vietnam and the subsequent withdrawal significantly reduced U.S. credibility as a potential protector of Thailand. In the meantime, other Southeast Asian countries began to assert themselves, providing one of the alternatives the Thai were seeking. Already in 1961, Thailand joined Malaysia and the Philippines in a loose grouping called the Association of Southeast Asia (ASA). When Singapore and the Southeast Asian giant, Indonesia, joined, the expanded organization was renamed ASEAN, officially inaugurated by the "Bangkok Declaration" of 1967. So far, it is very much less than a treaty organization for mutual defense. Nonetheless, it creates a sense of security and might be the seed for a much stronger alliance which could include more countries in the future such as democratized Burma and Cambodia. (Brunai has already joined.) Although the influence of ASEAN as a group on international affairs is still very limited, it is actively involved in the search for a solution for Cambodia. Disturbances and riots in Bangkok in 1973 were followed by changes of governments in Thailand. In 1975, the Thai prime minister visited Beijing, resulting in the establishment of full diplomatic relations. In recent years, an important common interest for Thailand and China has been their opposition to Vietnam. As reported below, there seems to emerge a change in Thailand's attitude to Vietnam, at least on the tactical level.

THE ECONOMY

The feeling of reduced dependence on the United States has been further enhanced by the significant progress in the Thai economy. The crucial period which ushered in the transition of Thailand into a growing and modernizing economy was, roughly, from 1958 to 1973, during which there were stable, albeit not very democratic, governments under Field Marshals Sarit Thanarat (1958–1962) and Thanom Kittikachorn (1963–1973). The following period was impacted by a combination of externally originated factors, such as the oil shock, and internal political instability. This was reflected for a few years in an unprecedented (for Thailand) rate of inflation. But the process of economic growth has continued and even accelerated in the years since then.

Much of Thailand's economic activity has been export-oriented. In the past, the exports were primarily agricultural and mining products. The significant development over the last two decades is that Thailand has increasingly produced manufactured products, including various kinds of machinery. What is even more impressive is that such industrial products have become a growing part of export.

The earlier manufactured products were import substitutes, manufactured behind high tariff walls. These tariffs have been progressively lowered, making Thai products more competitive in both domestic and world markets. One of the most impressive aspects of current Thai manufacturing is the speed of adjusting to changes in market conditions at home and abroad. This is a very reliable indicator of a modernized market economy. For better or for worse,

Thailand has become part and parcel of the world market and the international community.

A logical extension of this integration into the world has been the vast extension of the tourist industry of Thailand in recent years. The Thai government has made a major effort in that direction. Accommodating tourists requires cultural adjustments. Exposure to tourists from diverse countries leaves a not-so-easy-to-measure, but nonetheless important, influence on the people of the host country. The main policy motivation has been, of course, the foreign exchange earnings and the expansion in employment opportunities.

Another kind of foreign exposure which has evolved in recent years is employment abroad by Thai migrant workers. Most such workers go to the Middle East oil-exporting countries. Other foreign labor markets, especially for females, tend to be in nearby Southeast Asian countries. Singapore has been an important destination, although some restrictions were imposed recently on foreign workers by the Singapore government. Like tourism, the main reasons the Thai government encourages migrant workers to work abroad are the expected foreign exchange earnings (in the form of remittances) and expanded employment opportunities. But in this case, again, an important by-product is the foreign exposure. This, too, is difficult to measure, but there are various indications that returning migrant workers bring back some new ideas both in consumption and in business.

Both the promise and the dangers of Thailand's increasing integration into the world's capitalist economy were dramatically demonstrated during the 1980s. In the words of a prominent Thai economist: "The 1980s will be recorded in Thai economic history as a decade of drastic economic change" (Akrasanee 1990). The 1980s constituted not only a change but also volatility. The impact of the second major OPEC "oil shock" of 1979 was severe. Growth rates slowed down, inflation rose to 19.7 percent in 1980 (extremely high for Thailand), and the international current account was negative (and still is). As this was followed by the decline in the prices of most commodities exported by Thailand in the early 1980s, the situation deteriorated even further.

The government had to take stringent measures, including devaluation of the currency, as well as credit control and the like. Partly as a result of good policies, and partly due to the changes in the world markets, Thailand's economic performance vastly improved during the second half of the 1980s. Between 1987 and 1990, Thailand had the fastest rate of economic growth in the world, averaging 11.5 percent per year. From available indications, this rate will be slower in

1991, probably about 9 percent, which might still be the highest in the world, given the current recession in many countries. It is not surprising, therefore, that Thailand began to be regarded in some circles as the emerging new NIC (Newly Industrialized Country). This will depend, of course, on whether the expectations of continued growth in manufacturing, in industrial export, and in the GNP will materialize. There are some existing and potential bottlenecks. For example, there is a severe shortage of engineers and engineering students. Thai government missions and diplomatic posts around the world are seeking Thai engineers to offer them incentives to return home. Similarly, the capital market is still in an embryonic stage. Other bottlenecks are the deteriorating infrastructure facilities, inadequate capacity in oil refining and port facilities, and the like. In addition, the growth in manufacturing and its export is tied to a very large dependence on imported raw materials, parts, and oil, which are major contributors to the negative current account mentioned above. It is Thailand's very success that creates some doubts about future economic performance. There has been increasing dependence on foreign investment and financing. Some of these foreign sources have recently expressed doubt whether the high rate of growth is sustainable. The recent coup d'etat (see below) also may cause concern, especially among those who were already wavering when it occurred.

Nonetheless, it is clear that Thailand has passed the point of no return. It cannot go back. This does not only refer to the measurable economic performance. The economic changes were accompanied by a social, political, and cultural transformation that has touched even the inhabitants of remote villages which were previously inaccessible. The historian David K. Wyatt maintains that this is not what Generals Sarit and Thanom had in mind when they initiated the transformation (1984:290).

THE BUSINESS CABINET

The most important change in Thai public life has been the significant, but not complete, decline in the strangle hold which the military and the bureaucracy had over Thai politics since 1932. In that year, military officers and some intellectuals conducted a by-and-large bloodless coup reducing the king from an absolute to a constitutional monarch. Since then, most governments were headed by military men. Although the process of change has had its ups and downs, it took a significant change in 1982, when the new premier became responsible to the Parliament. This was the first time it happened since 1976 and the period before 1973. During the short three years after the 1973 student revolt, there were nonmilitary-controlled governments, but these did not last long, and the period ended with another military takeover.

When, after the 1988 elections, the former Premier, Mr. Prem, decided not to seek renomination to the premiership, a new premier was chosen from among the elected members of Parliament. The new government did not have a majority in Parliament and had to rely on a coalition of parties. Although the new Premier, Chatichai Choonhavan, was not entirely an outsider, having been a member of the military establishment, he certainly introduced new ideas, which some even considered revolutionary, in both internal and external policies. His conduct reminds one of some boisterous politicians in Western-style democracies. For example, he raised the minimum wage, stood up to the Americans, and made his first priority the extension of Thailand's business opportunities at home and abroad.

The military has still remained in the picture, though. The Army's Commander in Chief, General Chaovalit, redefined the role of the military to include participation in, and initiation of, civilian development projects. Many suspected that he had political ambitions, but it is very significant that he did this in ways that curry favor with the voters rather than using the old ways of taking power by force. Apparently, the potential political challenge made Mr. Chatichai and his advisers apprehensive. This fear increased in 1990 and ended up with the Cabinet removing General Chaovalit from his military post, thus presumably cutting him off from his power base. As we will see below, this was not the end of the story.

One of the most dramatic indicators of both the internal and external transformation of Thailand under Chatichai was its new policy toward its Indochinese neighbors. The Prime Minister, General Chatichai, said, "We have accepted that our common enemy these days is poverty. We must help the people to live a good life. Battles should be over because countries, big or small, are no longer at war." What this meant, in practice, was that Thailand's businessmen wanted to be at the ground floor with investment and trade in and with Laos, Cambodia, and Vietnam.

Instead of continuing with the unsuccessful border skirmishes with Laos, Thailand sent trade and good-will delegations. Mr. Chatichai himself headed a mission to Laos in November 1988 only three months after assuming the premiership. It resulted in agreements on a number of issues, including development projects in Laos. The declaration quoted above was made in February 1989 when the Premier of Laos paid a return visit to Thailand. That visit further advanced the cooperation between the two countries.

A similar move was made toward Vietnam. In mid-January 1989, a very large Thai delegation went to Hanoi, headed by the Thai foreign minister. That visit was of much greater significance because Vietnam is much larger and stronger than Laos. For centuries it was regarded in Thailand as a dangerous challenge; it is even more dangerous now that it also has a huge war-tested military. It still has substantial control over Cambodia with which Thailand has a long turbulent border. It also has troops and political presence in Laos. Thailand obviously had these facts in mind.

The new trend became even clearer when, in the same month, Mr. Chatichai invited to Bangkok the Vietnamese-backed Cambodian Premier, Hun Sen. This was a major departure from long-standing Thai policy and was done without consulting Thailand's friends, including the other ASEAN members. In retrospect, this move helped the progress toward a possible solution of the Cambodian question as evidenced by the meeting of all four Cambodian factions in Jakarta in early September 1990.

For perspective, it might be mentioned that relations with the United States, on the other hand, have shown signs of strain. These technically revolve around the removal by the United States (as of July 1, 1989) of Thailand from preferential treatment on eight Thai exports. The Thai consider such moves a retaliation for their refusal to bend to U.S. pressure. The United States, on the other hand, thinks it has been very patient with Thailand's refusal to take measures to protect U.S. copyrights and to allow American goods more access to Thai markets.

Such a conflict is a new phenomenon in Thai-U.S. relations, but it reflects the changes in the circumstances. The Vietnam War is over; Thailand has become a major exporter, and the United States is increasingly concerned about the deficit in its trade balance. What surprised some observers was the stridency on the part of Thailand. This is not the way Thais are supposed to behave, certainly not toward Americans. The United States and its citizens have had a very long and friendly relation with Thailand, but it was an unequal relationship where the Americans were like big brothers who provided guidance, training, aid, and the like. Could it be that there is a psychological element here as well? Could it be that the supposedly happy Thais felt less than comfortable with the unequal relationship? None of this means that the United States will not continue to be a major factor in Thailand's foreign relations and trade. It is still Thailand's largest trade partner and American corporations are major investors in Thailand. The largest number of Thai students in any country are in the United States. There is also a fast expanding Thai community in the United States. No precise number is available but they have a significant presence, especially in southern California. This is an entirely new phenomenon. There were never Thai communities abroad except for very few high-class families. (The current king was born in Cambridge, Massachusetts.)

A TEMPORARY REVERSAL

If proof was needed that Thailand's transition to democracy still has a way to go, it came in the form of a military coup on February 23, 1991. It was completely bloodless, as were most coups in Thailand, and followed a pattern familiar from the past. Also according to pattern, the coup leaders abolished the constitution and promised elections under a new constitution. The claimed reason for the coup was that the ousted government was corrupt, which might be true. But, then, past military-run governments were quite corrupt as well.

Another given reason was that the government was antimilitary, which might be objectively true in the sense that the stronger the economy and the business class are, the less politically relevant the Army becomes and the smaller its control over resources. Since the military controlled most Thai governments since 1932, it is not surprising that it is not particularly happy about this trend. Moreover, the ousting of General Chaovalit was interpreted by many in the military as proof that the Chatichai Cabinet was against them.

A third reason given was that the Chatichai government was plotting against the royal family. It is not at all clear what evidence there is to support such a claim. Nonetheless, such accusations can stir a substantial amount of emotions in Thailand. This aspect is particularly important because a crucial factor determining whether a coup succeeds or fails is the reaction of the king. There were a couple of coup attempts during the preceding premiership of Mr. Prem. Their failure is generally ascribed to the king's visible backing of Mr. Prem.

In this latest coup, the king was in a secondary palace in Chiang Mai in the North of the country, far away from the capital. Initially, he remained there, which, in the past, signaled his disapproval. However, later reports suggested that he insisted on revisions in the new constitution and that, subsequently, he went along with the new government.

The most important aspect of the coup is the very fact that it took place at all. It means that the very significant economic changes that have taken place during the last three decades have not yet resulted in enough social and political change so as to eliminate the viability of a coup as a method of changing governments. The above notwithstanding, there is little doubt that the country will continue to move toward freer citizenry. The fact that the king (and his advisers) went along with the coup at this day and age might not necessarily bode well for this form of monarchy in the long run after the present, very popular king leaves the scene. Some would argue, for example, that to the extent that the Chatichai government was guilty, it could have been charged in court or voted out of office by the elected Parliament. Obviously, time may not yet ripen for these approaches.

In the meantime, while the new government is in power (and there is no way of telling how long that might be), a number of policy changes could be noted. The most notable are in foreign relations. The new regime is likely to improve relations with the other ASEAN members. What irritated the latter included Chatichai's cuddling of the Communist regime in Pnam Penn and its sponsors in Hanoi. This, some ASEAN members thought, encouraged Hun Sen's government in Cambodia to refuse a temporary U.N. administration of the country as a step advancing the proposed peace plan.

At the time of writing, it is not entirely clear what other policies the new government will follow. It is not likely to change the fundamental direction of the economy, for example, since the new government is composed mostly of well-known technocrats.

Foreign investors might feel uncertain as a result of the coup, but in all likelihood, unjustifiably. In fact, the new regime announced soon after the coup that it would abide by all contracts signed by the preceding governments. The bigger damage was the effect on the domestic scene since some people will despair of ever having a true democracy in Thailand. Of course, as is explained below, it is not realistic to expect an exact replica of a Western-style democracy in such a culture. But an increasing number of Thais would like to have a life free of the fear and shame of military coups, bloodless though most of them have been.

THE BROAD BACKGROUND

Relating the important current facts and opinions, as has been done here, still leaves some fundamental aspects of Thai life unexplored. Although the casual observer might not be aware of it, their ethnic background and Theravada Buddhism are of great importance to the Thai. The question as to whether, how, and how much modernization and economic development would change these attitudes is far from certain.

Present-day Thais are, or at least consider themselves to be, a part of a larger group of people called Tai. Besides Thailand, Tai people can be found in Northeast Burma (the Shan states), Laos, North Vietnam (around the Dien Vien Phu area), and in South China. Until recently, it was thought that all Tai came from South China, where they had a kingdom which was destroyed by the Mongolic invasion. There now are some doubts whether this is the whole story. Whatever the exact history, there is little doubt that all these branches have a common linguistic and ethnic origin. Almost all of them are Theravada Buddhists, unlike Chinese and Vietnamese who, to the extent they follow Buddhism at all, are practicers of the Mahayana version.

Every Thai male is expected to spend at least a few months in a monastery as a monk. Everybody is expected to give alms to monks and monasteries. Important families spend large sums of money for funerals of their members, complete with memorial books and elaborate and expensive funeral structures which are then burnt with the corpses. This substantial sacrifice of resources is a well-entrenched part of the culture.

Theravada, which is the more straightforward or narrow version of Buddhism, is a guide to behavior. In practice, it is combined with folk culture and, for the upper echelons of society, with Brahaminism. Until recently, the common interpretation of Buddha's teachings did not favor business activities. As long as most of the commercial activities were done by the Chinese and other non-Thais, that apparent mismatch was not particularly relevant. But as more and more ethnic Thai become involved in business activities, the issue is bound to arise, and some new interpretations would have to come up. This issue is not entirely new. Already during the first half of the nineteenth century, King Mongkut, both before and after ascending to the throne, initiated reforms in Buddhist practices. Some believe these were inspired by Western ideas brought over by Protestant missionaries (Keyes 1987:182). We cannot presume to say what form the reconciliation might take, but we would like to leave the reader with the realization that the Thai take Buddhism very seriously and that it permeates almost all activities and social life. One cannot understand Thai behavior without due attention to this factor.

Since the non-Thai Burmese and Cambodians are also Theravada Buddhists, it might facilitate better relations in the future. This is by no means certain, since these people fought fierce wars in the past. In fact, Bangkok was established as the capital city because the former one, Ayuthaya, was completely destroyed by the Burmese during the late eighteenth century. Nonetheless, it is a very important bond. For example, the occasion of the visit of the Prime Minister of Laos mentioned above was a major Buddhist celebration in Northeast Thailand.

Since most of the exposure to foreign influence has been taking place in Bangkok, it is natural that changing attitudes and modes of behavior will occur earlier and be more acute there than in the rest of the country. But Thailand is a very centralized country. Practically all changes come from Bangkok, and the government's authority is very widely accepted. Through various instrumentalities, the government spreads the ideas and services throughout the country.

A good example of the government's role is the very successful campaign to reduce the rate of population growth. It is difficult to imagine such a success without the government. This refers not only to the resources required to pursue the campaign but, very significant in the case of Thailand, also to the prestige of the government. We have already pointed out how the nature and degree of modernization in Thailand traditionally have been regulated and screened by the government. Most Thais consider such government involvement natural. It might be pointed out here that, both in Japan and in "The Four Tigers" (the very successful NICs of East Asia), government involvement has been substantial. Some scholars believe that the single most important factor in economic development is the commitment of the government leadership to the cause (Syrquin 1988: 207–208). Since the Thai government is so committed, the prospects for continued economic and social progress are very good.

CHAPTER 9

The Ambiguities of Modernization:
The Political Class and Regime Change
in the Philippines

Albert Celoza

In the modernizing societies of East Asia, some segments are more involved in the official political life of the nation than others. This is the political class. They may be either obstacles or trailblazers of modernization, a key force for stasis or change within society. The political class often embraces Western ideas, while the rest of the polity is less affected by and derives fewer benefits from this movement away from traditional values and behavior. As a result, the political class usually is more integrated into the larger world than other groups in their country, whose views are more circumscribed by families and villages.

Because the state in Asia plays a major role in socioeconomic change, it is highly dependent on the political class. In this role, the political class supports the state in its interventions, and, in return, the policies of the state tend to redound to their benefit first. The authority of the state is supported by the political class as long as the regime is thought able and ready to affect changes that enhance their interests. State authorities, be they the reformist monarchs of Thailand, Chulalongkorn and Mongkut, Suharto of Indonesia, or Marcos and Aquino of the Philippines, need and benefit from the political class, which can determine the rise and fall of regimes.

Who makes up the political class? In the Philippines, they are the commercial landowning and business people, the managers of bureaucracy (both civilian and military, as well as public enterprises or government corporations), provincial and local elites, and local agents of foreign business interests.

In general, these elements of the political class share several basic characteristics. First, in developing societies where social economic distribution is highly unequal, members of this class make up a small, interrelated elite. Since the economy is still predominantly agricultural, landowners are also the leaders of business and commerce. With accumulated capital from farming, plantation owners branch out to other ventures. Since they have interests to protect, money to spend for campaigns, and resources to dole out as favors, they also tend to be active in local and national politics. This political power also preserves and enhances their economic dominance.

Second, members of the political class possess one or a combination of resources: machinery and technology, education and ideas, and financial capital. In particular, this sector of society is educated. Their education further ensures their social mobility and their influence and access to government service and policy-making.

Finally, the political class usually is the most Westernized sector of society. It consumes Western cultural norms and values, even though it may be highly ambivalent about this. Because of their education, access to media, and their more frequent interaction with the foreign sector, members of the political class imbibe Western and modern standards. They are the role models for the population for bringing into the country foreign ideas, habits, and patterns of consumption.

This chapter is a case study of the role of one political class in the political and economic modernization, or lack of it, of the Philippines. In particular, I will focus on the rise and demise of the regime of Ferdinand Marcos in the Philippines and the rise of Corazon Aquino. Ferdinand Marcos won the 1965 election. Such elections had been held every four years since the Philippines gained its independence from the United States. Though the transplant of American government institutions may have been imperfect at best, there was widespread support for the established system, which had allowed transfer of power as prescribed in the 1935 Philippine Constitution. Though elections did not necessarily change government policies, they transferred the helm of government from one political party to another.

Below the presidency, power rested on the regional elites. These *hacienderos* (landowners) often served as governors and members of Congress and exercised tremendous economic and political influence. The largely feudal socioeconomic structure of the provinces was held together by patron-client networks.

The late 1960s was a period of political ferment for Philippine society. The country experienced passionate nationalism and the worldwide trend of student activism. The electors voted a convention to amend the Philippine constitution, which was now perceived as a product of American colonialism. This refashioning of the political system responded to nationalist aspirations and the need for social reform.

There were demonstrations and riots in the cities. In the countryside, an incipient Maoist rebel movement was founded from the coalition of the Huk movement and the new leadership of the Communist Party, though the latter did not pose a threat to the established government in Manila. Although demonstrations denouncing bureaucratic capitalism and U.S. imperialism were perceived as nuisances to social order, their presence indicated fundamental problems in Philippine society. There were bomb threats to public buildings and an attempted ambush of the secretary of defense.

Marcos used these events as a pretext to abolish habeas corpus and to impose martial law on September 23, 1972. His regime was supported by the network of patron-client relationships, civilian and military bureaucracies, technocrats, business cronies, and provincial officials loyal to and favored by Marcos. With the strong backing of this group, martial law became a mechanism for instituting a permanent authoritarian government. The supporters of Marcos' rule hoped that the imposition of martial rule would calm the political disturbances, curb crime, and truly bring the "new society" that Marcos promised. There was only one violent incident that occurred during the imposition. When the military took over the broadcasting station owned and operated by the *Iglesia ni Kristo* (Church of Christ), the Bishop's guards fired on them. Prospective opponents of Marcos' takeover were arrested and incarcerated; when the situation settled, some of them were freed. The rest of society went about its business as usual. No tanks rolled in the streets. Martial law was even called the "smiling martial law." There were violations of human rights and civil liberties, acts of torture, and killings. People viewed these as limited to dissenters and rebellious elements.

THE BUREAUCRACY:
A KEY ELEMENT OF MARCOS' SUPPORT

The centerpiece of the process of directed development is the Philippine bureaucracy, which gathers necessary information, sets goals, and plans and implements strategies.

Unlike the political and constitutional structures of power of Philippine government, the bureaucracy did not experience drastic changes after imposing martial law. Marcos did issue General Order No. 1, which placed under himself the operations of the entire Philippine government. Bureaucratic reform was carried out without personnel changes, but merely the reorganization and expansion of the scope and responsibility of existing structures. Corruption is a frequent complaint against the bureaucracy, especially during elections. A purge was conducted to weed out the notoriously undesirable persons from government service in 1975. The purge list included those who had long since died, retired, or who had moved out of their offices. Those with political connections were able to escape the process.

As soon as martial law was imposed, slogans were broadcast in the media: "*Sa ikauunlad ng bayan, disiplina ang kailangan* (Discipline is a requirement of national development)." Government took over all forms of communication: information technologies, television and radio stations, newspapers, shortwave radios, citizens' bands, and even mimeographing machines. All publications were suspended until martial law authorities gave them a clearance. A Cabinet position was established to disseminate development goals and to mobilize the people to support the process. The government's media arm published information and produced programs ranging from agriculture to a documentation of the daily activities of the Marcos couple. Writers and publishers were pushed to censor themselves. Bureaucrats and government officials were expected to lead and disseminate the country's progress and were required to receive training on development and on the new society. Programs were provided to public servants ranging from central government employees to *barangay* (village) leaders. Government officials had to take such courses before they were permitted to travel abroad.

New social technologies also were introduced, such as project evaluation, integrated area and regional development, statistical analysis, survey techniques, zero-based budgeting, and other corporate and management tools from the United States. As development planning was institutionalized, the economic planning body was converted from a small office to a ministry with Cabinet rank and a cadre of newly hired economists, demographers, and statisticians.

At the helm of Philippine bureaucracy were the technocrats. Characterized as "professionally qualified advocates of modernization, equipped with vision, committed to economic rationality, and . . . convinced that planned intervention in the market is a condition for economic development" (Milne 1982:405), technocrats were graduates of U.S. universities and had experience in both business and academic fields such as engineering, economics, and business administration. They supported the use of planning and other technical tools in the management of government bureaucracy. Thus, they welcomed the unhindered operation of bureaucracy and the abolition of Congress. The prospects for implementing ideas free from political impediments was attractive to the technocrats. They were given the reigns of development planning and administration.

Because of their association with the West, the new class of experts lent prestige and credibility to the authoritarian regime. However, Marcos and other political leaders maintained control while the experts provided rationales for government policies. The technocrats did not pose a challenge to the regime but served as its instruments, supporters, and allies. They were politically weak since they did not have any political base, were mostly based in metropolitan Manila, and were confined to the central bureaucracy. They were clients in the patron-client network because they owed their influence to the regime.

Philippine bureaucracy grew in size and function as the centralized mechanism for authoritarian rule. More resources were generated through increased foreign borrowing to sustain government's growth. Philippine foreign debt grew to $25 billion. In addition to the luxurious ways of the Marcos family, monies were spent for patronage. During elections and referendums, salary and benefits increases were announced, and village leaders were given funds for local projects.

In spite of the rhetoric for decentralization, policy decisions were enacted centrally. Political authority did not devolve but radiated from the center during the Marcos years. According to Carino, "local governments tend to be mere extensions of the central government except where the local official [was] strong enough or his territory rich enough to take up the task of running his own programs" (1983:10).

The central bureaucracy strengthened its position and scope with the increase of image building projects. Philippine leadership wanted to be perceived as a leader of the Third World, spearheading the process of modernization. Thus, several five-star hotels were built for the 1976 International Monetary Fund (IMF) and World Bank conference. The Philippines also hosted the conferences on world law, tourism, and the United Nations Conference on Trade and Development. The Philippine International Convention Center also was built. The Philippine government invited the General Assembly of the United Nations to meet in Manila in 1977 and promised to shoulder its expenses, though the invitation was turned down. The government also built the Cultural Center, the Folk Arts Center (for the Miss Universe Pageant), and a film center (to host an international film festival similar to the Cannes). A basilica was even to be built on the occasion of Pope John Paul II's visit and the silver wedding anniversary of the Marcoses. The regime sponsored the Ali-Frazier boxing match, world chess competitions, and visits by celebrities in order to publicize the Philippines and integrate it into the modern world.

The changing skyline of Manila became a testament, if not to modernization, at least to the expanding class of modernizers.

THE MILITARY IN POLITICS

Even before the imposition of martial law, Marcos gave the military a prominent and expanded role. In his first State of the Nation address, he aimed for "increased training, new equipment and heightened morale . . . the need for reforming the nation's police forces, activating a Philippine Coast Guard, and expanding the military's socioeconomic development program" (Hernandez 1979:206–207). The armed forces became involved in civic action: infrastructure projects, agriculture, food production campaigns, education, and health. (This expanded role is similar to Indonesia's doctrine, *dwi fungsi* [dual role] for the military.)

Since Marcos' early days in Congress, he had established good relations with graduates from the Philippine Military Academy and junior officers, most of whom were already senior officers during Marcos' presidency. There was a marked increase in the number of officers and enlistees from Marcos' home province, and during the martial law period, eighteen out of twenty-two generals in the Philippine Constabulary and all of the top military command were Ilocanos (Canoy 1980:20). Ties of family ethnicity and patronage ensured their loyalty and support. Two top military leaders were related to Marcos. The chief of staff was Major General Fabian Ver, who concurrently headed the intelligence apparatus as well as the presidential security forces. Vying for top leadership was the deputy chief of staff, who was also chief of the constabulary and the national police, General Fidel Ramos, a graduate of West Point and more acceptable to U.S. military circles than Ver, who had been Marcos' chauffeur and personal henchman.

Increased aid from the United States made possible increased officer training and interaction with their American counterparts. The United States Agency for International Development (USAID) emphasized programs in public safety and internal security. Police and armed forces officers were sent to the United States for training, and technologies were provided to update communication, data collection, and administration of law enforcement. Total U.S. military aid from 1964 to 1971 is estimated at $631.7 million. In addition, the U.S. General Accounting Office reported that assistance to the Philippines had been augmented by the use of regular U.S. military personnel and equipment. Five military teams were assigned to help the Philippines in training, supply, maintenance, and equipment operation (Shalom 1981:110).

Marcos considered the military as partners of the civilian bureaucracy and in attaining national goals by maintaining "an atmosphere conducive to the development process" (Marcos 1974:3–4). The military was rewarded with salary increases and privileges, as well as enhanced power and prestige. They became dispensers of patronage, and, to some extent, they replaced traditional politicians. According to Harold Maynard, "Ordinary civilians, as well as families of military men, now regularly call upon senior officers to plead assistance in getting jobs, solving family problems, processing applications, securing community development projects, or replacing inept local officials. . . . Scenes which used to take place in the offices of senators and congressmen are increasingly taking place in the offices of generals and colonels" (1976:436). Through their connections, they were able to cut through red tape and facilitate transactions of their clients and constituents. When military officers reached retirement age, either their appointments were extended or they were appointed to key positions in the civilian bureaucracy and public enterprise.

Marcos characterized the armed forces as a "catalyst for social change," a "training institution for national leaders," the "defender of the seat of government," a "nation builder," and a "model of discipline and self reliance" (Maynard 1976:337). In return, the armed forces accepted authoritarianism as the most efficient instrument to progress devoid of disorder as well as democracy. In addition, martial law indoctrinated the military's sense of self-importance and messianic mission. During the Marcos era, they became more politicized and have remained so, ready to save the nation if political leaders do not perform to their satisfaction, and are willing to ally with political groups which they feel will act according to their interests.

THE ROLE OF BUSINESS

The Marcos regime actively exploited business and private industry as a basis of patronage. During his reign, Marcos rewarded close friends and supporters with government contracts and oligopolistic control of market sectors. In return, business owners served as regional leaders of the *Kilusang Bagong Lipunan* (New Society Movement), Marcos' umbrella political group.

These policies tended to concentrate national wealth in the already narrow oligopoly. Only 6 percent of Philippine business had public stocks while the rest is concentrated in eighty-one families (Doherty 1982:30). These families can be categorized into three groups. The first were the traditional elite that endured through the martial law years and did not suffer the fate of the Lopezes and Jacintos who lost their wealth: Ortigas, Laurel, Zobel-Ayala, Soriano, and Madrigal. The second were premartial law elite whose wealth grew significantly under the Marcos regime, such as Aboitiz, Elizalde, and Concepcion. The third group were those who accumulated wealth during the martial law years: Benedicto, Enrile, Cuenca, and of course, Marcos, and Romualdez.

Quite significantly, only the Jacintos and Lopezes, whose properties were taken over by the government in the national interest, suffered the onslaught of martial law while the rest survived and were significantly sheltered and supported by the regime. (The Lopezes are already back to the Philippines after the installation of Corazon Aquino to power.) Those who accumulated vast sums of wealth during martial law years owed their strategic position to Marcos and, in return, supported him. Eduardo Cojuangco, a sugar planter and cousin of Corazon Aquino, was supported by Marcos when he campaigned for Congress. He expanded his enterprise all over the country in coconuts, fishponds, cacao, and more sugar plantations, and also became chairman of San Miguel Corporation, a Philippine brewery.

Through a presidential edict, Cojuangco controlled the coconut industry through the Coconut Federation, a mandatory organization for farmers. The federation was to collect levies to stabilize coconut prices and production. The levies were also intended to fund benefits, insurance, and scholarships for planters. These monies were used mainly to purchase the United Coconut Planters Bank (UCPB) and the United Coconut Mills, the former was a bank owned by the Cojuangco family, while the latter was a company that controlled 85 percent of the coconut milling industry, also through presidential decree.

Juan Ponce-Enrile shared the administration of the coconut industry with Cojuangco and was chairman of the UCPB, Unicom, and Cocofed. At the same time, he was Marcos' minister of defense, customs commissioner, and secretary of justice. He owned farmlands in Isabela, timber logging concessions, and a match manufacturing company, and was director of the Construction Development Corporation of the Philippines (CDCP), a company owned by Rodolfo Cuenca, another crony of Marcos.

CDCP was formed in 1966, the year Marcos was inaugurated as President. One of its stockholders was Marcos' secretary of public works. Because of the connections, CDCP was awarded huge government contracts like the building of Manila North Expressway and the collection of tolls for this project for forty years. Later, CDCP became involved in overseas operations and established a shipping company. It incurred $100 million of government guaranteed loans, and when it became unprofitable, the government of the Philippines took over as the official container ship owner to the West Coast of the United States. Marcos also ordered banks to convert CDCP loans to equity. According to a confidential U.S. Embassy study entitled "Creeping State Capitalism in the Philippines," the Development Bank of the Philippines owned or managed seventy-three private concerns after it had converted their loans and loan guarantees to equity.

The regime's active involvement in business gave it the means to reward its supporters. Not only was the coconut industry monopolized, but the sugar industry, another main exporter, also was given to Marcos' fraternity brother, Roberto S. Benedicto. In addition to overseeing the sugar monopoly, Benedicto was ambassador to Japan, president of the Philippine National Bank, owner of television and radio stations, and of shipping lines that controlled Philippine-Japanese trade. A Japanese corporation was provided sugar mills with government financing, in return for which it paid Benedicto $6 million per mill. Despite the slump in the sugar market, modern equipment was installed with the proper payoff.

THE ROLE OF FOREIGN BUSINESS IN DOMESTIC POLITICS

U.S. business interests welcomed Marcos' imposition of martial law. It was widely believed that the first letter of congratulations to the President was sent by the U.S. Chamber of Commerce in Manila stating that they wished him every success in his endeavor to restore peace and order, business confidence, and economic growth, and that they assured him of their continuing confidence and cooperation (Bello 1981:8). Marcos was perceived as a friend of business because of the policies he made clear after the imposition of martial law: no nationalization or expropriation and the extension of parity rights to own land and maintain executive positions. Marcos hoped that multinational corporations would establish regional headquarters in the Philippines; thus, he exempted their foreign personnel from a number of regulations and taxation. By 1981, there were already about 200 active multinational company headquarters in the Philippines that fully supported government efforts to attract more firms to do the same.

To prospective foreign oil explorers, Marcos said, "We'll pass the law you need—just tell us what you want" (Shalom 1981:176). To further induce foreign investment, he banned strikes in pursuit of industrial peace and tried to keep wages low as a matter of government policy. The Central Bank of the Philippines Report for 1980 stated that "real wages for skilled workers were 63.7 percent and for unskilled workers 53.4 percent of what they had been in 1972" (Diokno 1981:28).

In 1980, when the lifting of martial law became imminent, the business sector expressed concern that "favorable conditions for economic expansion" will not continue (*Business Day*, December 23, 1980).

Marcos had hoped to produce another Asian economic miracle by pursuing a development policy reliant on foreign investment and capital. The United States accepted Marcos' priorities and excused his disregard for individual rights and democratic institutions. Increased power seemed necessary to ensure stability as well as the U.S.-Philippine patron-client relations (U.S. Congress, 1973:45).

THE COALITION OF REGIONAL AND LOCAL LEADERS

Marcos connected himself to the grassroots through recognized local and regional leaders. For example, he had as his Defense Minister Juan Ponce-Enrile, the influential leader of Cagayan Valley (Region 2), the Romualdezes in Leyte, the Duranos in Cebu, and Ali Dimaporo in Lanao. They represented the Marcos government in their respective provinces by distributing favors to their constituents before elections and referendums to guarantee favorable results for the regime.

There were around thirty powerful families scattered throughout the archipelago that had been the key to success of all political regimes (*Far Eastern Economic Review*, September 14, 1989:36ff.). They control rural banks, rice milling, trading stores, fishponds, trucking and shipping, ice-making plants, logging, land, and public offices. As such, they were and still are an indispensable link between the central government and the populace. It also was to their advantage that the Manila government remain attuned to their needs and those of their constituents. Marcos rewarded them with political positions by appointing them provincial governors, town mayors, and members of the *Kilusang Bagong Lipunan* (a quasipolitical party/movement under Marcos' leadership). Marcos integrated them into the national polity even as they maintained power in their respective fiefs. In effect, Marcos accorded legitimacy and official titles to their feudal positions.

Marcos could not have succeeded in maintaining authoritarian rule from 1972 to 1986 without the network of support of the political class. As much as they were responsible for his rise, they were also significant participants in his regime's decline and fall. Whoever is in power will have to deal with them.

THE POLITICAL CLASS AND REGIME CHANGE

In the mid-1960s when Marcos was first elected President, the Philippines had one of the highest per capita incomes in Asia, and it accounted for roughly 7 percent of the region's exports. Twenty years later, the GNP did not grow but declined; previous years of economic growth had been completely lost (World Bank 1987:57). Inflation surged from 10 percent in 1983 to 50 percent in 1984. The value of the peso declined, and unemployment and underemployment increased. There was massive capital flight, an indication of overall pessimism and loss of trust in the regime and the economy.

These deteriorating economic conditions, coupled with the assassination of Marcos' chief political rival, Benigno Aquino, triggered massive protests. The tragic event of 1983 showed the vulnerability of even one of the most powerful families in the country. Daily demonstrations, rallies, and protests were held, especially in Makati, the financial capital and bastion of wealth in the Philippines.

Marcos called a presidential election to prove that he still had the support of the people. It took many months of negotiations to unite the opposition under one banner. While the politicians were wrangling for the presidential nomination, much of the political sector was gathering in support of the opposition. Corazon Aquino, Benigno Aquino's widow, emerged as the presidential candidate. In her team were advisers with media and political connections with the United States. Because she provided hope to the business class whose interests were suffering due to the stagnant economy, an organization led by businessmen, the National Movement for Free Elections, was mobilized to guarantee that elections were kept honest. This organization also had the support of U.S. interests. With the help of U.S. media consultants, the campaign was played on American television. During the campaign, Mrs. Aquino was able to rouse a mass following. However, this did not translate to electoral victory because Marcos controlled the balloting, reporting, and the tallying process. After Marcos was finally ousted, the military admitted to committing fraud and intimidation. Its leader, Secretary of Defense Enrile, also admitted to jacking up votes for Marcos in his home region, Cagayan. Blatant fraud also was documented by massive international media coverage.

In protest, Aquino claimed victory and led demonstrations and civil disobedience. What directly caused Marcos' ouster, however, was the revolt of the military reform leaders in February 1986. The rebel soldiers and officers who encamped themselves in the armed forces headquarters were eventually joined by other elements of society. This revolt, called the people power revolution, was confined to the metropolitan Manila area in an area adjacent to military headquarters, post neighborhoods, government offices, shopping centers, and other symbols of privilege and modernity. Its participants were not peasants in remote areas, but urban dwellers. Their leaders were from the clergy, military, business, academia, and the opposition; that is, largely from the traditional political sector. The leftists did not participate as a group. The struggle was for the control of television and radio stations, not of strategic mountain passes. The rural populace was not immediately affected by the four days that unfolded in front of television cameras. Television viewers in the United States were fed minute-by-minute coverage of the fall of the Marcos dictatorship and saw more of it than millions of people in the rural Philippines.

Marcos fled the Philippines via American transport to exile in Hawaii, and Aquino was sworn into office. Because of her dramatic rise to power, Aquino enjoyed tremendous national and international popularity. The Philippine story was played like the triumph of the good over evil. Aquino provided new hope and optimism for change, as illustrated by the stock market. "While a dollar's worth of an average stock at the beginning of 1986 rose 23 cents by the end of the year on Wall Street, 22 cents in London or even $1.12 on the Madrid bolso, the same investment would have generated a $2.40 profit in the Philippines (*The New York Times*, March 16, 1987:30). The country registered some growth, and inflation was curbed. Aquino appointed Cabinet leaders who are advocates of the free market. Their background was similar to the technocrats of the Marcos years. Some of them were owners and managers of business themselves who left the private sector to join the new government. Their economic program consisted of the dismantling of monopolies created by Marcos, privatization, and the creation of a hospitable business environment for local and foreign investors. Regional leaders and provincial elites quickly shifted their allegiance to Aquino with the exception of some leaders in Northern Philippines, Marcos' birthplace.

Like Marcos, Aquino considered land reform essential. Marcos even called it the "cornerstone of the new society" but did not implement a credible program. Similarly, Aquino and the revived Philippine Congress enacted a comprehensive agrarian reform program, but their legislation was weak and continued to protect the traditional landowning class, most of whom are in Congress, like the Aquino family itself.

The current Aquino government is constantly threatened by military coups. The military's support has not been constant and strong despite Aquino's efforts to win it. She raised soldiers' salaries, retired Marcos' favored generals who had passed their retirement age, and promoted colonels who had been frozen in rank. She also invited dialogue and reconciliation with the left. A faction in the military perceives that she has not exercised strong leadership. More than this, they believe that they can lead the national effort better themselves. They have sympathizers among politicians and business leaders.

Just as Marcos needed the political class to maintain himself in power, Aquino is vulnerable without their support. The rift within the political class that helped bring Aquino to power also created perceived instability and shaken business confidence. Aquino's authority, as well as that of her successors, depends on the continued support of the political class. Given the ambiguous commitment of this class to full democracy and an open market economy, the modernization of the Philippines will likely remain ambiguous as well.

CHAPTER 10

China in the Pacific Regional Economy

Gavin Boyd

Under an economic reform group headed by Deng Xiaoping, China's modernization program has been directed toward building a system of market socialism with elements of guided capitalism. The growth strategy has aimed increasingly to be led by exports. Rigidities in the heavily bureaucratic command economy are intended to be gradually overcome by developing a more autonomous and efficient government structure, by freeing enterprises from administrative controls, and by the phased ending of price controls. Manufacturing at rising technological levels, primarily for advanced countries, has been intended to finance imports of capital goods. These goods would increase the industrial capacity for more competitive exporting, while reducing dependence on revenue from sales of commodities in those markets.

Late entry on the path of export-led growth that has been taken by the East Asian NICs, however, has made it difficult for China to compete for U.S., Japanese, and West European markets. The export performance of Chinese firms, moreover, has been negatively affected by persistent administrative controls established under the command economy and by slow price liberalization, as well as by inadequate development of the economic infrastructure. Stronger administrative controls over enterprises and markets recently have worsened these problems. This has reflected a shift of power to conservative elite groups whose influence had increased in reaction to problems resulting from partial economic liberalization during the mid-1980s. Inflation, serious shortages of consumer goods, profiteering, and unemployment had tended to discredit the economic liberalization program.

A further shift of power to conservative elite groups followed the student demonstrations for democracy in late May 1989. This has resulted in stronger emphasis on administrative control of the economy and on political discipline, which indirectly dampens prospects for growth. The student demonstrations dramatized the potentially destabilizing effects of economic liberalization, since it was clear that the rationale for that policy had weakened the credibility of the ideology and the role of the Communist Party, especially by making explicit the need to reduce the party's involvement in government and in enterprise. Concerns of the leadership about threats to the stability of the regime were no doubt increased by reports of unrest precipitated by Gorbachev's reforms in the USSR and of the growth of popular pressures for reform in East European states. Elements in the leadership favoring continued economic liberalization were evidently very disadvantaged because that policy, in the minds of uncommitted, as well as conservative, elite groups, was associated with the general deterioration of political discipline and party control which had prepared the way for the student demonstrations.

A fundamental issue for the conservative group now in control is how to promote technocratic modernization with strong political discipline that will ensure the maintenance of their regime. Emphasis on self-reliant industrialization can be increased but only within limits set by the country's backwardness and with the probability of slow progress. The absorption of Western and Japanese technology and management methods, which can ensure faster industrialization, also involves cultural interactions that have generally influenced Chinese academics, officials, and management personnel in a liberal direction over the past decade. Reliance on imports of technology from the USSR is not satisfactory for several reasons: the Soviet Union's own technological lag, the virtual unconvertibility of its currency, and its restricted market for Chinese manufactures. Moreover, any expansion of economic ties with the USSR risks greater openness to information about events linked with Gorbachev's reforms and about popular demands for more representative government in Eastern Europe.

The current emphasis on strong government, political discipline, and economic stabilization can be expected to continue, since the conservative leadership group appears to draw support from within the military elite and higher levels of the party. The status and interests of the military establishment had been affected for several years by economic liberalization and also, apparently, by some reduction of military influence in high level policy-making. Public official declarations about the importance of curtailing indoctrination and organizational activities in the interest of economic reform also had affected the Communist Party's status and interests.

The combination of stricter administrative controls and economic stabilization will tend to aggravate problems in the regime's partially liberalized economy. Managers of enterprises will be obliged to operate more cautiously because of increased administrative and party supervision, the prospect of new price controls, and the risks involved in developing links with foreign firms. The quality of administrative guidance and control of the economy is likely to remain low because of a new emphasis on political qualities in staffing government organizations and widespread discrimination against officials considered to have been supporters of the former leadership and its policies of liberalization. Management will seek to reduce risks and demonstrate achievements in the new environment by securing official favors for financing, procurement, and marketing. However, this will tend to restore many of the features of a command economy, including bureaucratic inertia and technological lags.

Chinese firms will, thus, tend to lack interest in foreign markets, and those which were more export-oriented will find it difficult to compete. A capacity for medium and higher technology manufacturing aimed at Pacific and other markets will be lacking. The regime's dependence on revenue from exports of low-technology products and commodities, thus, will remain very substantial. Meanwhile, deficiencies in competition against exports of products by the East Asian NICs, especially South Korea and Taiwan, will increase as firms in those trading states continue to strengthen their comparative advantages. Chinese enterprises may continue to benefit from linkages with foreign firms, but managements will be reluctant to accept the risk of such connections, and foreign corporations are likely to remain cautious.

China is on the periphery of a Pacific pattern of trade and transnational production. This pattern is dominated by high volume commerce and cross investment between the United States and Japan. Ranking next are relatively large trade flows and international production links between the East Asian NICs and the United States and Japan. At a lower level are the more unequal economic links between Japan and the United States on the one hand, and the four large members of the Association of Southeast Asian Nations (Malaysia, Thailand, the Philippines, and Indonesia) on the other. These four states are at various stages of transition from import-substituting to export-oriented industrialization as they attempt to follow the developmental paths taken by the NICs. Chinese exports of commodities and low-technology manufactures compete mainly against these four ASEAN members.

A great volume of Japanese direct investment is tending to accelerate industrialization in Taiwan, South Korea, and Singapore. This investment also links these states more closely to Japan and, thence, to the global economy. The outflow of Japanese direct investment became very substantial after the appreciation of the yen and the depreciation of the dollar in 1985. The movement of this investment into the NICs will likely become even larger with greater regional economic cooperation. This prospect was opened up by the Baker initiative of 1989 to establish a consultative regional economic association in the Pacific.

ANALYZING TRANSITIONS FROM COMMAND TO MARKET ECONOMIES

Studies of change in China have to take into account the problems for reform-minded leaders, problems mainly associated with the mid-term costs and strains of policies of political and economic liberalization. In a sequence typical of Communist regimes, the reform leadership's coalition tends to be weakened by the economic and political disruptions that follow attempted reforms and that dramatize the dangers those reforms can pose for large numbers of officials whose careers are threatened. The emergence of reform leadership signifies some consensus that a regime is suffering from the dysfunctional effects of over-management, is failing to attain satisfactory economic growth, and is losing legitimacy because of pervasive criticism of its deficiencies and rejection of its ideology. A reform leadership has both personal and nationalistic motivations to promote drastic change. Personal power can be strengthened by removing conservative elites who have been discredited as sources of bureaucratic inertia and by elevating more qualified and more energetic technocrats to high posts. Improved administration can then promise increased overall growth and encourage more positive public attitudes. Widening policy consensus can then facilitate further removals of conservatives within the elite, while the staffing and restaffing of high level posts can prevent the formation of a stable secondary elite to which the top leadership might be accountable.

The basic principle of a reform strategy is the promotion of subsystem autonomy for general efficiency and welfare, under a leadership which identifies with subsystem interests and mobilizes them against a discredited administrative structure, thus offering new career opportunities and increased freedom. The principal risks are that increased autonomy for state enterprises, price liberalization, and attempts to reorient government functions will not sufficiently improve the economy, or at least not fast enough. If this happens, managers of enterprises will tend to seek security by continuing to operate as clients of supervising ministries. Managers and officials will be reluctant to identify fully with reform policies because of uncertainty about the future political power of the reform leadership. Market forces, moreover, will not be sufficiently freed to produce their intended effects. Instead of improved overall performance, then, strains in the economy, probably aggravated by administrative incompetence and noncooperation, will provoke social unrest and weaken the reformers.

A virtually unavoidable cost of a reform strategy is the rapid alienation of relatively large numbers of party and government officials marked for removal because of their association with prereform policies and patron-client networks, their lack of enthusiasm for administrative improvement, and their presumed incompetence. The insecurity felt by these officials tends to make them ready to support a high level drive for restabilization that can promise them safety. Meanwhile, they obstruct new and more qualified technocrats who may be appointed to senior posts because of foreign degrees and experience. Bureaucratic rigidity can thus increase because officials resist reform. Altogether, the Communist political economy is likely to perform less effectively after a reform drive has been launched than it did previously, that is, before pervasive official resistance and caution intensified established bureaucratic rigidities.

The mix and sequencing of reform endeavors and their context also affect their prospects. Emphasis on economic liberalization before political restructuring can be advantageous in a less-developed society. In China, this has been evident because liberalization in the large rural economy was an immediate success. Industrial changes to give increasing scope to market forces, however, have been very difficult to manage, and the negative consequences have affected the status of proposals for political reforms. A drive for political restructuring to prepare the way for economic liberalization can be appropriate in a more advanced Communist state because, in such states, liberalizing industrial measures would be difficult to manage without extensive administrative reorganization and restaffing. This is the main lesson evident in recent Soviet experience. Yet, political liberalization has substantial costs and can lose appeal because tolerance of limited pluralism, in effect, encourages disaffected groups to resort to direct action. Also, weaker economic performance tends to result from the destabilizing effects of the political reforms on administrative direction of the state enterprises.

The degree of elite confidence in the effectiveness of free market forces is critical in implementing policies of economic liberalization. When power is intensely personalized, however, as in China, the relevance of economic principles for policies tend to be much less. In an underdeveloped, strongly authoritarian state socialist system, moreover, leaders may not understand the functional significance of economic ideas that are alien to their own ideology. Furthermore, where there is much culturally-based emphasis on elite status and authority, as in China, policy-learning is likely to be limited. Difficulties in implementing economic reforms, due to bureaucratic incompetence and resistance, can, of course, further hinder policy-learning. Thus, leaders often fail to comprehend the problems associated with the transition to more prices and greater autonomy of enterprises.

No matter how they are sequenced, however, directing economic liberalization and controlling limited pluralism requires a combination of superior political leadership and technocratic management. The political leadership is needed to build elite coalitions that will counter possible erosions of support for reforms as problems of transition are encountered. Technocratic capacities are needed to cope with those transition problems, but their use will depend on the extent to which ideology can be revised to accommodate a political economy with extensive free enterprise and a state sector functioning in a market context.

The growth objectives of economic reforms entail shifts away from autarky toward substantial interdependence, with acknowledgment of economic backwardness and of the need for transfers of advanced technology. If conservative resistance to reforms terminates a program of economic liberalization, the regime will become less able to manage interdependencies competitively to improve its weak bargaining position. The political influences from economic interactions with advanced capitalist states also may encourage criticism of the conservative regime.

Analyses of such transitions thus have to take into account multidimensional causal processes. Caution has to be observed in assessing the policy-learning during those transitions because conservative resistance only increases after the stresses of economic liberalization become apparent and the basic logic of reform has been recognized. Numerous studies of China's economic reforms before mid-1989 carried a tone of optimism about continued policy-learning that showed insufficient awareness of the growing strength of conservative resistance to those reforms.

THE ECONOMIC REFORMS IN CHINA

In China the context of contemporary political and economic change has been unique; no other Communist regime has experienced an upheaval like the Cultural Revolution, which marked the last phase of Maoist rule. The drive for reform and for technocratic modernization sponsored by the post-Mao leadership was, to a large degree, a reaction against the destructive strife of that upheaval.

The agenda of issues was, in effect, set negatively by the severely adverse effects of the Cultural Revolution on the regime. There were manifest imperatives to restore order, prevent any continuation of despotic one-man rule, institutionalize a more representative form of elite power, and achieve rapid economic progress that would compensate for extraordinary failures of the last two decades of Maoism.

At first, the strategy of the post-Mao reform group headed by Deng Xiaoping successfully combined rural economic liberalization, multilevel coalition building, and restaffing of many branches of the government, party, and the military establishments. The rural economic liberalization required little macromanagement effort at the center, promoted rapid increases in farm output, and generated broad support in the countryside. The general restaffing was facilitated by encouraging hostility to officials who had prospered during the Maoist period and by rehabilitating victims of the Cultural Revolution, with whom Deng and his associates could identify, as they also had suffered in that purge. Appropriate conditions were, thus, established for economic liberalization in the industrialized urban areas.

Substantial change was difficult, however, because coalition building and restaffing on a much larger scale became necessary and required extensive reliance on personalized elite networks. There was a great need both for technocratic skills, even at middle and lower levels, and also for drastic retrenchments to eliminate overstaffing. Thus, many officials became insecure and resistant. Meanwhile, the promotion of enterprise autonomy and the decontrolling of prices in the industrialized urban areas were poorly managed. The markets, which were only partially liberalized, functioned inefficiently, with serious shortages and higher prices. Strong inflationary pressures developed, especially because of excessive lending by financial institutions. As the price increases became large, there was a proliferation of corrupt practices. Improvements in managerial and technical efficiency were difficult because the autonomy of enterprises remained low and because the market environment reflected uncertainties about supplies of inputs, administrative pricing policy, and the movement of liberalized prices.

The remedies to be anticipated from the further economic liberalization, which was advised by foreign experts and international organizations, were not endorsed by less reform-minded leaders to whom power began to shift as the regime's economic problems weakened the status of the modernizing elites. A growth of intra-elite pressures for restabilization through strengthened administrative economic controls was aided by unrest among educated young people. That is, their discontent appeared to demonstrate that economic liberalization was undermining the political foundations of party and government control.

The student protest of May 1989 reflected an acute weakening of the appeal of the official ideology. The justification of technocratic modernization had been that China was in a primary stage of social-ism and that, before progressing further, it would have to achieve a higher level of economic development by reintroducing capitalist methods of production and distribution. A clear but unacknowledged implication was that social control of the forces of production had been grossly dysfunctional and that these forces would have to be liberated through virtual privatization. This implication was made all the more evident by official encouragement of an entrepreneurial spirit, adoption of foreign capitalist methods of management, and efforts to attract foreign direct investment for joint ventures.

Thus, the formal justifications of the new modernization policy conflicted with a basic Marxist thesis concerning the need to liberate forces of production from capitalist constraints that thwart their development. This inconsistency further undermined the proposition concerning the primary stage of socialism. This was because the elements of ideology that the early reform leadership were endeavor-ing to preserve and reaffirm were associated with the discredited system of Maoist rule. Also, the projected superiority of the future stages of socialism was difficult to accept in view of the progress achieved by capitalist states from which China had to learn, as well as in view of Gorbachev's admission about the deficiencies of the more advanced form of socialism in the USSR.

Student disaffection from the regime and its official ideology also weakened the Communist Party's indoctrination work among young people; this trend was strengthened by the attractive career oppor-tunities opening up because of liberalization. Thus, the political psychology of the decline of ideology reflected both the conflicts between the new values of the younger generation and the Marxism-Leninism of the Maoist period, as well as the value conflicts manifest in the new official ideology discussed above. As a doctrine intended to legitimate the post-Mao authority structure and the drive for tech-nocratic modernization, this ideology was clearly of declining utility and offered little protection against the penetration of Western ideas about the necessary linkage of capitalism and democracy.

A pervasive effect of the decline of ideology—as it influenced offi-cials and the managements of enterprises—was the growth of cor-ruption. The persistence of bureaucratic rigidities meant that, in order to succeed, new business ventures had to secure official favors. Moreover, persons who extended these favors had the further incen-tive of keeping their fixed incomes up with or ahead of inflation.

Linked in various degrees with corruption was a proliferation of informal arrangements whereby enterprise managements, instead of developing entrepreneurial roles in the evolving market setting, collaborated with the administrative agencies from which they were intended to be freed. Managements retained strong incentives to preserve official connections that could assist them in acquiring investment funds, procuring inputs, and marketing products.

The drive for restabilization through stronger administrative control of the economy and through the imposition of greater political conformity after the student demonstrations aggravates the functional problems of the command economy that the post-Mao leadership had been attempting to remedy. In this process, long-standing cultural and institutional obstacles to modernization have become more significant, especially because a coherent doctrine of restabilization is absent.

CURRENT CHANGES IN CHINA

Under a new party leadership headed by Jiang Zemin, who had directed the party apparatus in Shanghai, the Chinese regime is committed to intensifying political education which, according to a speech by Deng Xiaoping, had been neglected over the past decade. Jiang Zemin was appointed Party Secretary General at a plenary session of the Party's Central Committee during the third week of June 1989. He replaced Zhao Ziyang, who was disposed following student protests for failing to oppose bourgeois liberalization while gravely neglecting the party's ideological and organizational activities.

The new emphasis on ideology is intended to foster dedication to a state socialist system under party direction. Officials are to make administrative controls more effective in the economy, and they are to receive more active cooperation from management and workers. Corrupt practices in the bureaucracy and in enterprises are to be diminished through intensified indoctrination and stronger administration. The practical significance of this is that elements of the technocratic elite who are identified with economic liberalization and thought to favor dialogue with student protesters are under suspicion. Thus, like their spokesman Zhao Ziyang, the technocratic elite may be victims of a purge that is believed to have begun at all levels. Official policy is to deal mercilessly with the counterrevolutionary elements who supported the student unrest.

The shift of power to hard-line bureaucrats will affect the quality of administrative performance, because many officials who have been given new powers have been chosen because of personal links with Zhao Ziyang's critics and opponent, and because of political rather than technocratic considerations. Many other officials who have remained in their posts must now support state control of the economy and avoid showing enthusiasm for any measures that might increase the scope for market forces. Concerns about personal security and career interests have presumably become very intense among these officials because of extensive restaffing. This insecurity is reinforced by widespread anticipation that intra-elite conflict will follow the death of Deng Xiaoping and may result in extensive purging.

The negative effects of this power shift on entrepreneurship in the state enterprises are increasing and are likely to increase further. This is because the greater economic difficulties caused by new administrative restraints on market forces will almost certainly generate further economic distress and, thereby, cause the present leadership to impose even greater control rather than to allow enterprise autonomy and freer price movements. A vicious circle can, thus, be envisaged, in which a drift toward the stagnation typical of a command economy causes authorities to aggravate the problems of overmanagement responsible for economic decline.

In the new context of intra-elite relations, with a cleavage between the hard-line elements committed to restabilization and the technocrats who had been cooperating with Zhao Ziyang's policies, a functional policy mix must be difficult to advocate. There is a hard-line bias against economic liberalization measures, based on beliefs that these would disrupt elite control and economic stability and contribute to political pressures for further bourgeois liberalization. In the priorities of the present leadership, resolute engagement with the latter danger is the primary task.

The generally depressing effects of the power change on entrepreneurship are likely to make the need for a functional policy mix all the more obvious; however, the dominant hardliners are concerned primarily with state power and do not appear to be influenced by, or to possess a sophisticated understanding of, the dynamics of market socialism. Presumably, there is now reluctance to take an interest in the recent experiences of East European countries and an unwillingness to seek guidance from research institutes that had been cooperating with the administration until mid-1989. Moreover, there are, no doubt, desires to avoid policy choices that would appear to reflect tacit agreement with measures introduced during Zhao Ziyang's period of leadership.

One can expect increases in the inefficiencies associated with a command economy, including low productivity, cumulative underspecialization, and failures to achieve effective interaction and exchange between enterprises. At a very fundamental level, technological problems have become more serious and are setting quite demanding requirements for the regime's policy-makers. Technology policy in recent years had been evolving toward economic liberalization and outward-oriented growth. Because such policy was being influenced increasingly by exchanges with Western and Japanese institutes, however, it is now under pressure to become more insular and to restrict interactions with foreigners. Purging and overregulation now hinder more innovative research and development. Also, the stimulus of an outward-oriented industrial policy, which previously was not very strong, is now even weaker.

Foreign direct investment policy in principle remains open. Inducements to attract such investment into resource extraction and manufacturing for export have been offered since the late 1970s; however, foreign firms have been discouraged by uncertainties about the regime's future, inadequate infrastructure, a lack of skilled labor, and the incompetence of the Chinese bureaucracy. All these factors have become more significant since mid-1989, and officials implementing foreign direct investment policy in the new context are understandably affected by the current vigilance against the penetration of bourgeois ideas. Before mid-1989, it appeared that attracting a larger volume of foreign direct investment could help to compensate for the inefficiencies of Chinese enterprises. However, managers of foreign firms now have to reckon with a more disorderly and uncertain business environment and less cooperative behavior by Chinese officials. The potential advantages of access to the Chinese market, moreover, have become more remote because the regime's overall growth rate is likely to remain at a low level for some years.

Foreign trade policy has evidently become a more vital element in the policy mix because of the increased difficulties of attracting direct investment by outside private firms. In principle, this policy continues to serve the building of a modern outward-oriented industrial establishment by financing technology imports through exports of commodities and low-technology manufacturers. Depressed commodity prices and Western, as well as Japanese, discrimination against low-technology imports have hindered this growth strategy since it began under the post-Mao leadership. Advancement into higher technology manufacturing for export has been the intended solution, but this has now become more difficult, not only because of the negative effects of economic restabilization on entrepreneurship and on domestic research and development, but also because of limited opportunities for linkages with foreign firms and reduced foreign business interest in the Chinese economy. In addition, competition against the East Asian NICs has become more demanding as their firms have increased their comparative advantages through very active entrepreneurship and faster commercialization of technological innovations, while operating in more supportive domestic policy environments.

With the new emphasis on administrative control of the economy, the bias in China against exporting is likely to become a more potent restraint on expanding external commerce, and this must be expected to have a significant effect on the performance of enterprises that hope to move into higher technology manufacturing for export. Managers who operate within the state-directed domestic economy desire secure access to subsidies and wish to avoid assessments of their performance in ventures into highly competitive and unpredictable markets. Commodities and textiles appear to constitute about 80 percent of the regime's exports to advanced countries. Thus, very large increases in manufactures at medium-technology levels will be needed over a long period before export-led growth comparable with that of the East Asian NICs will be possible. Substantial deficits are incurred in commerce with the major industrialized democracies. These are offset to a considerable extent by surpluses in trade with less-developed Third World countries. However, exports of manufactures to more-developed Third World countries are becoming more difficult as these markets are penetrated by the NICs and the industrialized democracies, especially Japan.

Fiscal policy has become more important with the shift to administrative restabilization. This is because enterprises with reduced autonomy operating in more restricted markets have become more dependent on state financing and, indirectly, on the state financing of firms linked as suppliers or consumers. Hence, the problem of soft budget constraints is tending to become more serious. The quality of central budget management also is probably deteriorating because of the power shift to less market-oriented decision-makers. This partially liberalized command economy is comprised of large numbers of relatively uncooperative budget-maximizing enterprises, burdened with over-management, and prone to excess investment. These problems tend to increase due to inadequate productivity. Fiscal discipline within the context of such a system is difficult to achieve and can offer only a partial solution unless the policy trend is reversed to allow more scope for market forces.

Inflation has been high in recent years because of fiscal expansion unmatched by productivity and because of loose monetary and financial policy in a context of weak markets. Currently, administrative power is being emphasized to prevent price increases, but it is not clear whether there will be sufficient efforts to introduce monetary and financial discipline. Implementing such efforts will be difficult because the shortage of competent officials, which was evident before mid-1989, is likely to become more serious as purging continues. Currency depreciation, which became necessary during the years immediately before the current phase of repression, will probably continue.

Altogether, macromanagement under the conservative leadership is tending to become an exercise in forceful restabilization. The consolidation of power, which involves much reliance on personal connections, is undoubtedly the dominant concern. Economic liberalization and political restructuring that had been proposed by Zhao Ziyang at the Thirteenth Congress of the Chinese Communist Party in late 1987 are now seen by the authorities as twin evils threatening the foundations of the regime. These fears have led to an intense effort to revitalize the party's efforts at political indoctrination. Administrative rationality is undermined by these attitudes and actions as enterprise managers, government officials, and party functionaries all tend to become more conservative and reactive.

CHINA IN THE PACIFIC ENVIRONMENT

Before the power shift in mid-1989, China was becoming more open to the international political economy on the basis of an outward-oriented strategy of growth. The most important relationship was with Japan, the main source of advanced technology, official aid, and private investment, and the main market for Chinese products. The United States ranked next as a trading partner and as a source of official aid and private investment. Developing market-economy East Asian states, in which overseas Chinese business communities were relatively large, were important markets for the regime's low-technology manufactures. Hong Kong was and, more quietly, continues to be an important economic partner, especially in the Pearl River Delta region of the Southeast.

Because of economic backwardness, relatively modest trade volumes, and a recent history of domestic strife and collaboration with the Communist guerrilla movements in Southeast Asia, China was on the periphery of a rapidly growing pattern of trade and transnational production that linked the NICs with Japan and North America. Developing a more active role in the pattern depended on advancing into higher technology manufacturing for export. It depended further on attracting large-scale Japanese and U.S. direct investment for export-oriented industrialization, and on securing developmental aid from international lending agencies, Japan, and the United States. China's emerging image as a state undergoing progressive internal reform also was helpful, but so were cultural and military resources that could be used for economic and political gain. Japan could be influenced through its cultural affinities with China. Market-economy

Southeast Asian states were interested in expanding trade with the Chinese in hopes of further declines in Chinese support for Communist insurgents.

In the present pattern of Pacific relations, the regime's economic links with Japan have become even more important. Japanese trade policy is less influenced by the moral considerations that encourage U.S. economic sanctions against China. The domestic political interests of the ruling Japanese Liberal Democratic Party, moreover, oblige it to strengthen relations with China to assist the strategies of Japanese firms to promote trade and investment.

Japan is now well-placed to expand its economic ties with China. These ties may develop on a scale sufficient to offset some of the tendencies toward slow growth caused by the Chinese regime's restabilization measures. For nearly two decades, the Chinese have looked mainly to Japan for large-scale credits to facilitate imports of technology. A high degree of interdependence has evolved as China had provided oil and raw materials in exchange for factories and machinery, as well as a growing volume of consumer goods. Chinese interest in Japan as the primary supplier of technology has been very active, moreover, because of Japanese official and business enthusiasm for such a relationship and also because China is often able to manipulate Japanese policy. Some years ago, the Japanese had to accept cancellations of major technology transfer contracts signed under an ambitious but poorly planned Chinese procurement policy.

In the mid-1980s, large imports of Japanese consumer goods resulted in a heavy trade deficit. Efforts to restrict imports from Japan and increase Chinese exports to Japan substantially reduced the trade imbalance. There was a hidden cost for Japan since increases in imports of Chinese low-technology products tended to limit increases in imports of such products from developing market-economy East Asian states seeking to cope with deficits in their trade with Japan. Strains in Japan's economic relations with those states thus remained somewhat more serious than they would have been had Japanese policy not given priority to Chinese demands for access to Japan's markets. Yet the scope for Chinese leverage on trade questions has remained limited because the low quality of many of the regime's products has tended to discourage consumer interest in Japan. The expansion of Japanese operations in global markets, moreover, especially since the appreciation of the yen in late 1985, has tended to draw Japanese corporate interest away from China to some extent. This trend may increase as Japanese firms position themselves in the integrating market of the European Community and observe caution in dealing with the new Chinese conservative leadership.

China is likely to emphasize securing technology from Japan because of the available Japanese credits. Such credits are likely to remain less restricted than those from the United States. Also, attracting more active Japanese economic interest is probably considered necessary in view of expected problems in the current restabilization phase. Interactions with Japan, moreover, are, no doubt, considered to involve fewer dangers of the bourgeois ideological penetration than those with the United States. Furthermore, there are major strategic considerations. China's interests would be affected if the USSR under Gorbachev's new economic policies were to become a more important focus of Japanese corporate and administrative attention. Also, the USSR might induce Japanese firms into ventures to exploit resources in the Soviet Far East.

China's relationship with Japan has an additional regional dimension because it has some influence on interactions between Japan and the United States. Japanese interest in the Chinese market involves competing against the United States. Also, the trade concessions that the Japanese make tend to obligate the United States to be more accommodating toward China, for example, on questions of exporting sensitive technology. The U.S. administration's interest in the Chinese market was demonstrated within a few weeks after the massacre of students in Peking in mid-1989 when economic sanctions were waived to allow sales of four passenger aircraft to the regime.

Interactions with the United States are not assisted by cultural affinities, as in the case with Japan, but have benefited from the U.S. administration's strategic concern to discourage any Sino-Soviet military cooperation and to assist the evolution of a Chinese regime oriented toward deepening involvement in the international economy. Advantages also are derived from U.S. administrative and corporate interest in the Chinese market. There also is scope for leverage to induce the U.S. administration to reduce its formal ties with Taiwan and to avoid actions which could enhance Taiwan's international status. The U.S. administration displayed little opposition to the suppression of the student protest in mid-1989 and has not helped Taiwan to extend its network of international contacts. At present, the main U.S. sanction against the hard-line Chinese authorities is to restrain the export of high technology, including some of military significance, and to defer support for loans to China by international lending agencies. The political will to maintain these moderate pressures may erode if Japanese and West European trade links with China expand significantly. For Chinese authorities, the relationship with the United States would then be more open to manipulation.

Before mid-1989, China's trade policy had benefited from significantly preferential U.S. treatment of the regime's textile market. It also had benefited from gradual relaxation of U.S. controls over the export of advanced defense-related technology to China, which had continued despite steadily expanding Chinese arms sales to Third World countries, including Iraq and Iran. For the present, Chinese access to the U.S. textile market has not been affected, but this may happen if legislative pressure on the U.S. administration for strong sanctions against China continues and if the Chinese authorities resort to provocative behavior. U.S. administrative controls on advanced-technology exports are likely to remain quite restrictive for the present but could be gradually moderated if overall relations improve.

On the Chinese side, relating to the United States requires much political skill to secure substantial economic and strategic benefits while preventing the penetration of bourgeois ideology. The authorities emphasize vigilance to exclude such ideology; this is especially evident in a more restrictive policy on academic and scientific cooperation and on social interaction related to business and official contacts. Although the United States' economic sanctions and its efforts to postpone loans to China by international lending agencies are not provoking strong hostility, neither have they lessened the repression of dissent that initially provoked these U.S. measures. The Chinese authorities may consider U.S. interests outside a bilateral relationship, and the Cambodian issue provides an important opportunity for this. For several years, China has helped to build the military capabilities of the Khmer Rouge, using supply routes through Thailand. The Chinese military establishment has been actively involved in this, and its influence in overall policy-making has probably become stronger since the hard-line political leadership asserted its control. China probably wishes the Khmer Rouge to regain control of Cambodia after a Vietnamese withdrawal. However, an interim strategy which could ostensibly meet U.S. hopes for a different outcome would not be difficult to implement and could promise some reciprocity by the United States. The Khmer Rouge could remain the most powerful force in Cambodia under an administration that would appear to be sufficiently representative for U.S. observers; the Khmer Rouge then could gain control after that administration had been in place for some time.

In addition to possible temporary consideration of U.S. concerns relating to Cambodia, Chinese policy may be influenced by hopes of expanding economic and political ties with Southeast Asian countries which were being strengthened while Zhao Ziyang was in office. Indonesia and Malaysia have opposed Thailand's collaboration with China's military support for the Khmer Rouge and have favored continuing Vietnamese control in Cambodia insofar as this has been a barrier to Chinese expansionism. The hard-line Chinese leadership, however, may wish to impose more respect for its power in the region; accordingly, it may ignore the political advantages of a compromise settlement in Cambodia that would allow the Khmer Rouge to take control only after some delay.

Outside Indochina, the hard-line leadership gives much attention to member states of the Association of Southeast Asian Nations. Most of these states have shown little concern about the massacre of student demonstrators in Peking. The established policy of expanding commercial and political ties with the Association's members appears to be continuing, in part to limit opposition to a Cambodian settlement that would provide obvious benefits for China, and in part to compete against Soviet initiatives, since the USSR has sought to establish a stronger political and economic presence in the area. Advantages for China are derived from the relatively low level of cohesion between the Association's members and from their failure to initiate any substantial economic cooperation within their grouping.

Commercially, China is linked with ASEAN members through Hong Kong and apparently, to a lesser extent, through Singapore. Roughly 25 percent of China's exports go to Hong Kong, and undetermined proportions of these are shipped to Malaysia, Thailand, the Philippines, Indonesia, and Singapore. Direct exports to Singapore— about ten times less in value than those to Hong Kong—also include large volume of items that are re-exported from Singapore to other Southeast Asian countries. Direct exports to the Association's principal members other than Singapore are in the $200 to $300 million range and constitute relatively small items in the foreign trade of these states, which is oriented toward Japan, the United States, and the European Community.

Economic inducements can have only modest significance in China's relations with ASEAN members. To the extent that this is evident to the hard-line leadership in Peking, a need may be seen to project Chinese power more effectively in the area, not only to secure acceptance of demands relating to Cambodia but also to induce greater consideration of China's regional interests. These interests, it must be stressed, include limiting the Soviet presence in Southeast Asia and avoiding a secondary role for China in a Soviet-sponsored scheme for arms control in the Pacific. Because the U.S. administration gives priority to interactions with the USSR, there is a strong incentive for the hard-line leader to assert themselves in the East Asian strategic balance as a means of ensuring greater attention in U.S. policy.

PROSPECTS FOR THE FUTURE

The evolution of the Chinese regime and of its involvement in East Asia and the Pacific is being determined principally by interactions within the conservative ruling group, and between that group and the remainder of the elite. Conflicts over methods of restabilization may be tending to divide the ruling group, and it may also be divided by succession struggles after the death of Deng Xiaoping. Both moderate economic sanctions imposed cautiously by the United States and U.S. restraint in critical communications may be contributing to additional intra-elite divisions.

Rivalries deriving from organizational interests and diverging ideological as well as policy perspectives will probably develop between party, administrative, and military elite figures. Political restabilization requires more active party influence in the government, with corresponding reduction of overall systems efficiency. The military elite, previously obliged to accept a restricted political role, will tend to benefit from differences between the administrative and party figures. It may not only assert its influence in policy-making, but also acquire more responsibility for maintaining internal order. A return of public security forces to military control, from which they were removed several years ago, would signal more active involvement by the military in consolidating the authority of the new administration.

Intra-elite divisions will tend to hinder decision-making on economic and political issues. The choices regarding economic and political restabilization will remain difficult. If a strong leader emerges, there may be energetic engagement with the tasks of overall restabilization. For the present, however, the pattern of intra-elite relations suggests that factional rivalries will prevent that and tend to obstruct resolution of the succession issue. The new Party Secretary General, Jiang Zemin, has lower status in national affairs than Li Peng, who, as Chairman of State Council, formerly ranked below the Party's Secretary General, Zhao Ziyang. The leading role which the party is intended to have in the regime's affairs, however, makes the post of Secretary General more important than that of the top government figure. Questions of relations between the party and the government, thus, are likely to be prominent in the rivalries between factions.

U.S. policy, which allowed the resumption of large-scale investments in China within three months of the suppression of the pro-democracy demonstrators, will probably be increasingly influenced by hopes of gradually strengthening the positions of the technocrats in the Chinese leadership who recognize the importance of expanding economic ties with the advanced capitalist states. Such technocrats, if they gain a stronger role in policy, may be linked with the domestic political restabilization policy. The overall effect on the Chinese leadership could involve some moderation of the outlooks of the conservative elements as well as a shift in the power balance to favor more liberal technocrats. Alternatively, conservative elements could be provoked to reassert the prime importance of ideological struggle to prevent the bourgeois cultural penetration associated with the growth of U.S. economic presence in China, especially if U.S. firms entering through direct investment become significantly more numerous.

The U.S. economic policy is linked with U.S. efforts to strengthen political and defense ties with China, which may continue to be directed against Russia. Complex opportunities for manipulating the relationship will remain open for the Chinese and will assist bargaining with Russia. Using the U.S. interest in economic, political, and defense cooperation without relaxing the repression of dissent and the ideological struggle against foreign bourgeois ideology may gain recognition as a viable policy. Opposition to market-oriented change will probably remain strong because of the perceived potential of such change to destabilize the regime and undermine the party's control.

In the Pacific regional economy, China will benefit from improved economic ties with the United States. It will benefit even more from strengthened links expected with Japan. But China will remain seriously disadvantaged by the inefficiencies of Chinese firms and their weakness in foreign markets and by a home economy experiencing over-management, purging, and pressures for ideological conformity.

The inefficiencies and difficulties of Chinese firms will be aggravated by the economic stabilization policy for several years. Even if this policy is moderated, its effects will continue to dampen entrepreneurship, slow the development of infrastructure, increase volatility in the imperfectly controlled markets, and multiply uncertainties about regulatory policies and measures. All these problems require managers to use personal connections, which contribute to the persistence of clientelist practices in the government and party. The profitability of an enterprise in such a setting will, of course, be difficult to judge in real terms and will not be a guide to export capacity, which, in any case, will have a lower priority.

In the Pacific regional economy, then, China will remain peripheral longer than would have been predicted had the previous economic liberalization policy continued. The growth of high-volume commerce and transnational production linking Japan and the United States will continue, and U.S. government borrowing to cover the federal deficit will continue to depend heavily on Japanese investment decisions. Member states of ASEAN will continue to become more closely tied to the Japanese and U.S. economies, especially through attracting Japanese direct investment for medium and higher technology manufacturing directed at the U.S., Japanese, and local markets. Taiwan and South Korea also will become more closely connected with the U.S. economy and, to a lesser extent, with Japan's, with less pronounced asymmetries and, increasingly, on a basis of intra-industry commerce. This entire pattern is moving to higher levels of specialization, interdependence, and technological progress, with the expansion of Japanese, U.S., and developing East Asian multinationals. In contrast, the Chinese economy is evolving at a slower pace, with numerous built-in biases against outward-oriented industrialization.

References

Abe, Yasuji. 1980. *Ginko-Shoken Ronso Oboegaki*. Tokyo: Nihon Keizai Shimbunsha.

Adams, John. 1982. "Money Market Mutual Funds: Has Glass-Steagall Been Cracked?" *Banking Law Journal* 99:4–54.

Aikman, David. 1986. *Pacific Rim: Area of Change, Area of Opportunity*. Boston: Little, Brown and Company.

Akrasanee, Narongchai. 1990. "TDRI 1989 Year-End Conference on Thailand in the International Economic Community." Bangkok: Thailand Development Research Institute.

Alberti, R., and S. Castiglioni. 1985. "Politicae Ideologia en la Industrializacion Argentina." In *Boletin Informativo Techint* 239. Buenos Aires: Techint.

Arrighi, Howard. 1979. *Organizations and Environments*. New York: Prentice-Hall.

Ayal, Eliezer B. 1969. "Thailand." In Golay F., Pfanner M., Anspach R., and Ayal E. (eds.), *Underdevelopment and Economic Nationalism in Southeast Asia*, pp. 267–340. Ithaca, N.Y.: Cornell University Press.

–––. 1962. "Thailand's Six Year National Economic Development Plan." *Asian Survey* 1:33–43.

–––. 1961. "Some Crucial Issues in Thailand's Economic Development." *Pacific Affairs* 36:157–164.

Aziz, Sartey. 1978. *The World Economy and Japan*. Tokyo: The Japan Institute of International Affairs.

Balassa, B. 1988. "The Lessons of East Asian Development, An Overview." *Economic Development and Cultural Change* 36, 3 (Suppl.).

Barret, Richard, and Soomi Chin. 1987. "Export-Oriented Industrializing States in the Capitalist World System: Similarities and Differences." In Frederic C. Deyo (ed.), *The Political Economy of New Asian Industrialism*, pp. 23–43. Ithaca, N.Y.: Cornell University Press.

Becker, Gary. 1983. "A Theory of Competition Among Pressure Groups for Political Influence." *Quarterly Journal of Economics* 98:377.

Bello, Walden, and Elaine Elinson. 1981. *Elite Democracy or Authoritarian Rule*. Manila: Nationalist Center.

Berger, Peter L. 1987. *The Capitalist Revolution: 50 Propositions on Liberty and Democracy*. New York: Wildwood House.

Calder, Kent. 1989. "Elites in an Equalizing Role: Ex-Bureaucrats as Coordinators and Intermediaries in the Japanese Government-Business Relationship." *Comparative Politics* 21 (July 1989):379–404.

———. 1988. *Crisis and Compensation: Public Policy and Political Stability in Japan, 1949–1986.* Princeton: Princeton University Press.

Canitrot, Adolfo. 1981. "Teorfa y practica del liberalismo. Politica antiinflacionaria y apertura economica en la Argentina, 1976–1981." *Dessarrollo Economico* 15, 59 (October-December):331–352.

Canoy, Reuben R. 1980. *The Counterfeit Revolution: Martial Law in the Philippines.*

Cargill, Thomas, and S. Royama. 1987. *The Transition of Japanese Finance and Monetary Policy in Comparative Perspective with the United States.* Stanford: Hoover Institution Press.

Carino, Ledivina V. 1983. "Administrative Accountability: A Review of the Evolution, Meaning and Operationalization of.a Key Concept in Public Administration." Commission on Audit Professorial Lecture.

Castells, Manuel. 1984a. "The Shek Kip Mei Syndrome: Public Housing and Economic Development in Hong Kong." Paper delivered at the seminar on the *Urban Informal Sector in Center and Periphery.* The Johns Hopkins University.

———. 1984b. "Small Business in a World Economy: The Hong Kong Model, Myth and Reality." Paper delivered at the seminar on the *Urban Informal Sector in Center and Periphery.* The Johns Hopkins University.

Chai, B. Karin. 1990. "Phoenix Rising from the Ashes: Status and Prospect of the Labour Movement in Hong Kong." Paper delivered at the 8th Biannual Conference of the Society for Asian Australian Relations. Brisbane.

Chan, Gordon Hou-Sheng. 1985. "Taiwan." In John Dixon and Hyung Shik Kim (eds.), *Social Welfare in Asia.* London: Croom Helm.

Chang, In-Hyub. 1985. "Korea, South." In John Dixon and Hyung Shik Kim (eds.), *Social Welfare in Asia.* London: Croom Helm.

Cheek-Milby, Kathleen, and Miron Mushkat. 1989. *Hong Kong: The Challenge of Transformation.* Hong Kong: Hong Kong University Press.

Chen, Edward K. Y. 1979. *Hyper-Growth in Asian Economies: A Comparative Study of Hong Kong, Japan, Korea, Singapore, and Taiwan.* New York: Holmes and Meier.

Cheng, Tun-Jen. 1986. "Political Regimes and Development Strategies: Korea versus Taiwan." Unpublished manuscript.

Choi, Jang-Jip. 1985. "The Strong State and Weak Labor Relations in South Korea: Their Historical Determinants and Bureaucratic Structure." Paper presented at the Conference on the Dependency Issue in Korean Development: Comparative Perspectives. Seoul.

Chow, Nelson W. S. 1985a. "Hong Kong." In John Dixon and Hyung Shik Kim (eds.), *Social Welfare in Asia.* London: Croom Helm.

———. 1985b. "Welfare Development in Hong Kong—The Politics of Social Choice." In Y. C. Jao et al. (eds.), *Hong Kong and 1997, Strategies for the Future,* p. 477ff. Centre of Asian Studies, Hong Kong: Hong Kong University Press.

Clark, C. 1987. "Economic Development in Taiwan: A Model of Political Economy." *Journal of Asian and African Studies* 22, 1/2:1–16.

Cummings, Bruce. 1987. "The Origins of Development of the Northeast Asian Political Economy: Industrial Sectors, Product Cycles, and Political Consequences." In Frederic C. Deyo (ed.), *The Political Economy of the New Asian Industrialism*, pp. 44–83. Ithaca, N.Y.: Cornell University Press.

Curtis, Gerald L. 1971. *Election Campaigning, Japanese Style*. Tokyo: Kodansha International.

Davies, Steven N. G. 1989. "The Changing Nature of Representation in Hong Kong Politics." In Kathleen Cheek-Milby and Miron Mushkat (eds.), *Hong Kong: The Challenge of Transformation*. Hong Kong: Hong Kong University Press.

———. 1977. "One Brand of Politics Rekindled." *Hong Kong Law Journal* 7, 1:44–79.

Deyo, Frederic C. 1989a. *Beneath the Miracle: Labor Subordination in the New Asian Industrialism*. Berkeley: University of California Press.

———. 1989b. "Labour Systems, Production Structures and Export-Manufacturing: The East Asian NICs." *Southeast Asian Journal of Social Science* 17, 2:8–24.

———. 1987. "State and Labor: Modes of Political Exclusion in East Asian Development." In Frederic C. Deyo (ed.), *The Political Economy of the New Asian Industrialism*, pp. 182–202. Ithaca, N.Y.: Cornell University Press.

Diokno, Jose W. 1981. *Justice Under Siege: Five Talks*. Manila: Nationalist Center.

Di Tella, Guido. 1985. "Rents, Quasi-Rents, Normal Profits and Growth: Argentina and Areas of Recent Settlement." In D. C. M. Platt and Guido Di Tella (eds.), *Argentina, Australia and Canada: Studies in Comparative Development, 1876–1965*, pp. 37–52. New York: St. Martin's Press.

Doherty, John. 1982. "Who Controls the Philippine Economy: Some Need Not Try as Hard as Others." Working Paper. University of Hawaii, Manoa.

Dornbush, R., and Y. C. Park. 1987. "Korean Growth Policy." Mimeograph. Economic Planning Board.

Economist Intelligence Unit. 1983. *Hong Kong: Economic Prospects to 1987*. Special Report, No. 156. London: The Economist.

Eisenstadt, Shlomo N. 1985. "Cultural Traditions, Power Relations and Modes of Change." In O. F. Borda (ed.), *The Challenge of Social Change* 32, pp. 9–38. London: Sage Publications.

Emmons, Charles F. 1985. "Public Opinion and Political Participation in Pre-1997 Hong Kong." In Y. C. Jao et al. (eds.), *Hong Kong and 1997 Strategies for the Future*, p. 53ff. Centre of Asian Studies. Hong Kong: Hong Kong University Press.

Evans, Peter. 1989. *Dependent Development*. Princeton: Princeton University Press.

———. 1987. "Class, State, and Dependence in East Asia: Lessons For Latin

Americans." In Frederic C. Deyo (ed.), *The Political Economy of the New Asian Industrialism*, pp. 203–226. Ithaca, N.Y.: Cornell University Press.

Feldman, Robert. 1985. *Japanese Financial Markets: Deficits, Dilemmas and Deregulation*. Cambridge: MIT Press.

Haggard, Stephan. 1987. "The Politics of Industrialization in Korea and Taiwan." In Helen Hughes (ed.), *The Success of East Asian Industrialization*. Sidney: Cambridge University Press.

Haggard, Stephan, and Tun-Jen Cheng. 1987. "State and Foreign Capital in the East Asian NICs." In Frederic C. Deyo (ed.), *The Political Economy of the New Asian Industrialism*, pp. 84–135. Ithaca, N.Y.: Cornell University Press.

Haggard, Stephan, and C. Moon. 1983. "The South Korean State in the International Economy: Liberal, Dependent or Mercantile." In John Gerald Ruggie (ed.), *The Antinomies of Interdependence*. New York: Columbia University Press.

Haley, John. 1986. "Toward a Reappraisal of the Occupation Legal Reforms: Administrative Accountability." Manuscript. University of Washington School of Law.

Hamilton, Clive. 1986. *Capitalist Industrialization in Korea*. Boulder, Colo.: Westview Press.

Henderson, Jeffrey. 1989. "Labour and State Policy in the Technological Development of the Hong Kong Electronics Industry." *Labor and Society* 14.

Hernandez, Carolina G. 1979. "The Extent of Civilian Control of the Military in the Philippines: 1946–1976." Ph.D. dissertation. State University of New York at Buffalo.

Hirschman, Albert O. 1981. *Essays in Trespassing*. New York: Cambridge University Press.

Hofheinz, Roy. 1982. *Eastasia Edge*. New York: Basic Books.

Hong Kong, Social Welfare Department. 1989. "Changes in Social Security Provisions in Hong Kong." *Asian News Sheet* 19, 2 (June).

Horiuchi, Akiyoshi. 1984. "Economic Growth and Financial Allocation in Postwar Japan." Discussion paper (August). Research Institute for the Japanese Economy, University of Tokyo.

Horiuchi, Akiyoshi, F. Packer, and S. Fukuda. 1988. "What Role Has the 'Main Bank' Played In Japan?" *Journal of Japanese and International Economics* 2:159–180.

Hoselitz, B. F. 1989. "Industrialization and Urbanization." In C. F. Dreyers (ed.), *The City as a Centre of Change in Asia*. Hong Kong: Hong Kong University Press.

Hoshi, T., A. Kashyap, and D. Sharfstein. 1990. "Bank Monitoring and Investment: Evidence from the Changing Structure of Japanese Corporate Banking Relationships." In Glenn Hubbard (ed.), *Asymmetric Information, Corporate Finance, and Investment*. Chicago: National Bureau of Economic Research.

Hsiao, Hsin-Huang Michael. 1986. "Development Strategies and Class Transformation in Taiwan and South Korea." Revised version of a paper presented at the Conference on Origins and Consequences of National Development Strategies (March). Latin America and East Asia compared. Duke University, Durham, N.C.

Hsueh, T. T., and T. O. Woo. 1989. "The Changing Pattern of Hong Kong-China Relations since 1979: Issues and Problems." Conference on the Future Development of Trade and Industry. Hong Kong.

Ichikawa, Nobuyuki. 1986. "Kigyo Kinyu no Kozo Henka wa Doko made Susundeiru no ka." *Kinyu Zaisei Jijo* (December 8):34–39.

The International Commercial Bank of China, Republic of China. 1983. "The Social Welfare System and Social Welfare Expenditures of the Republic of China." *Economic Review* November-December, 216:6–14.

International Labour Office. 1985. *Report of the Director-General: Application of ILO Standards*. Tenth Asian Regional Conference, December. Jakarta.

International Social Security Association. 1989. "ILO in Asia and the Pacific: A Review of Events and Activities in the Field of Social Security." *Asian News Sheet* 19, 2 (June).

Jao, Y. C. 1985. "The Monetary System and the Future of Hong Kong." In Y. C. Jao et al. (eds.), *Hong Kong and 1997, Strategies for the Future*, pp. 361–404. Centre of Asian Studies. Hong Kong: Hong Kong University Press.

Jao, Y. C., C. K. Leung, Peter Wesley-Smith, and S. L. Wong. 1985. *Hong Kong and 1997: Strategies for the Future*. Centre of Asian Studies. Hong Kong: Hong Kong University Press.

Johnson, Chalmers. 1989. "MITI, MPT, and the Telecom Wars: How Japan Makes Policy for High Technology." In Chalmers Johnson, Laura D'Andrea Tyson, and John Zysman (eds.), *Politics and Productivity: How Japan's Development Strategy Works*. New York: Ballinger.

–––. 1978. *Japan's Public Policy Companies*. Washington, D.C.: American Enterprise Institute.

Jones, Leroy P., and Il Sakong. 1981. *Government, Business, and Entrepreneurship in Economic Development: The Korean Case*. Cambridge, Mass.: Harvard University Press.

Kanamor, Hisau. 1980. *The World Economy and Japan*. Tokyo: The Japan Institute of International Affairs.

Karr, Frederick. 1979. "Is the Cash Management Account Innovative Brokerage or Unlawful Competition for Smaller Banks?" *Banking Law Journal* 96:307–312.

Katz, D. 1983. "Group Processes and Social Integration: A Social System Analysis of Two Movements of Social Protests." *Journal of Social Issues* 39:4.

Keyes, Charles F. 1987. *Thailand, Buddhist Kingdom as Modern Nation-State*. Boulder, Colo.: Westview Press.

Kim, K. S., and J. K. Park. 1985. *Sources of Economic Growth in Korea: 1963–1982*. Seoul: Korea Development Institute.

Kim, Kwan S. 1985. *Politica Industrial y Dessarrollo en Corea del Sur*. Mexico City: Nacional Financiera.

Kim, Kwang-Suk, and Michael Roemer. 1979. *Growth and Structural Trans-*

formation. Cambridge, Mass.: Harvard University Press.

Kim, Kyong-Dong. 1979. *Man and Society in Korea's Economic Growth.* Seoul: Seoul National University Press.

Kinyu. 1977. "Ginko to Yubinchokin no Keihi." (April):47–48.

Kinyu Zaisei Jijo. 1981. "Shin Ginko Hoan Ohaba Shusei." (April 27):14–16.

Koo, Hagen. 1987. "The Interplay of State, Social Class and World-System in East Asian Development: The Cases of South Korea and Taiwan." In Frederic C. Deyo (ed.), *The Political Economy of the New Asian Industrialism,* pp. 165–181. Ithaca, N.Y.: Cornell University Press.

―――. 1986. "Dependency Issues, Class Inequality, and Social Conflict in Korean Development." In Kyong-Dong Kim (ed.), *Dependency Issues in Korean Development: Comparative Perspectives.* Seoul: Seoul National University Press.

Korzeniewicz, Miguel. 1986. "The Influence of Foreign Direct Investment on Development Strategies: Argentina, Brazil, South Korea, Mexico, Taiwan." Unpublished manuscript. Duke University.

Kruger, Anne. 1985. "The Experience and Lessons of Asian Super Exporters." In Corbo et al. (eds.), *Export Oriented Development Strategy.* Boulder, Colo.: Westview Press.

Kuan, Dominic H. S. 1983. *Organizing Participatory Urban Services.* Hong Kong: Chinese University, Occasional Papers, No. 2.

Kuznets, Simon. 1988. "An East Asian Model of Economic Development: Japan, Taiwan and South Korea." *Economic Development and Cultural Change* 36, 3 (Suppl.).

Kwack, T. 1983. "Development Strategy and Investment Incentives: A General Equilibrium Simulation Analysis." *The Korea Development Review* 5:3 (December).

Lall, S. 1984. "Exports of Technology by Newly Industrializing Countries." *World Development* 12:471–480.

Lau, Siu Kai. 1985. "Political Reform and Political Development in Hong Kong: Dilemmas and Choices." In Y. C. Jao et al. (eds.), *Hong Kong and 1997: Strategies for the Future,* pp. 22–49. Centre of Asian Studies. Hong Kong: Hong Kong University Press.

Lau, Siu Kai, and H. S. Dominic Kuan. 1988. *The Ethos of the Hong Kong Chinese.* Hong Kong: Chinese University Press.

Lee, Joseph S. 1985. "Labor Relations and the Stages of Economic Development." *Industry of Free China* 71, 4 (April 25).

Leung, Benjamin K. P. 1990. "Collective Violence: A Social-Structural Analysis." In B. K. P. Leung (ed.), *Social Issues in Hong Kong,* pp. 143–163. Hong Kong: Oxford University Press.

―――. 1985. "Strategies for the Future." In Y. C. Jao et al. (eds.), *Hong Kong and 1997: Strategies for the Future.* Centre of Asian Studies. Hong Kong: Hong Kong University Press.

Leung, C. K., J. W. Cushman, and G. Wang. 1980. *Hong Kong: Dilemma of Growth.* (Eds.), Canberra: School of Pacific Studies; and Hong Kong: Hong Kong University Press.

Li, K. T. 1989. *The Evolution of Policy Behind Taiwan's Development Success.*

New Haven, Conn.: Yale University Press.

Lim, Hyun-Chin. 1985. *Dependent Development in Korea: 1963–1979.* Seoul: Seoul National University Press.

Litt, David. 1989. "Introduction of Commercial Paper in Japan: A Case Study of Financial Services Decision Making." Manuscript. University of Chicago Law School.

Liu, Paul K. C. 1988. "Employment, Earnings, and Export-Led Industrialization in Taiwan." *Industry of Free China* 70, 4–5 (November).

Marcos, Ferdinand E. 1974. "The Military and National Development." *Philippine Military Digest* 16, 2:22–37.

Maynard, Harold W. 1976. "A Comparison of the Military Elite Role Perceptions in Indonesia and the Philippines." Ph.D. dissertation. American University.

McCubbins, Mathew, and F. Rosenbluth. 1990. "Why Zoku? Explaining Japan's Extra-Parliamentary Policy Making Apparatus." Manuscript. University of California, San Diego, Department of Political Science.

Milne, R. S. 1982. "Technocrats and the Politics in the ASEAN Countries." *Pacific Affairs* 55, 3(Fall).

Morimoto, Tadao. 1979. *Ginko Daisenso: Hakaisuru Nihon no Kinyu Kozo.* Tokyo: Diamond.

Moxon, Richard W. 1980. *Dynamics of the Asia-Pacific Business Environment.* Seattle: University of Washington Press.

Nagatomi, Yuichiro. 1978. *Antei Seicho Jidai no Koshasai Shijo.* Tokyo: Okura Zaimu Kyokai.

Nakajima, Toshihiro. 1979. *Aru Ginko Gappei no Zasetsu.* Tokyo: Toyo Keizai Shimposha.

Nakatani, Iwao. 1984. "The Economic Role of Financial Corporate Grouping." In M. Aoki (ed.), *The Economic Analysis of the Japanese Firm.* Amsterdam: Elsevier Science Publishers B.V.

Ng, Margaret. 1989. *Truth Gets Buried between Lines.* SCMP.

Ng, Pedro. 1986. *Recent Trends in Work and Leisure in Hong Kong and Higher Education's Response.* Hong Kong: Chinese University Press.

Ng, Sek Hong H. 1987. *Report on the Working Conditions of Female Workers in Tsuen Wan District.* Hong Kong: Tsuen wan District Board.

Ng, Sek Hong, and Victor F. S. Sit. 1990. *Labour Relations and Labour Conditions in Hong Kong.* Geneva: United Nations International Labor Organization.

Niskanen, William. 1971. *Bureaucracy and Representative Government.* Chicago: Aldine.

Noguchi, Yukio. 1987. "Public Finance." In Kozo Yamamura and Yasukichi Tasuba (eds.), *The Political Economy of Japan: The Domestic Transformation,* pp. 186–222. Stanford: Stanford University Press.

Noll, Roger. 1983. "Government Regulatory Behavior: A Multidisciplinary Survey and Synthesis." In Noll and Owens (eds.), *The Political Economy of Deregulation.* Washington, D.C.: American Enterprise Institute.

Olson, Mancur. 1982. *The Logic of Collective Action.* Cambridge, Mass.: Harvard University Press.

Park, Chong Kee. 1975. "Social Security in Korea: An Approach to Socio-Economic Development." Research report of the Korea Development Institute. Seoul: Korea.

Pauly, Louis. 1988. *Opening Financial Markets: Banking Politics on the Pacific Rim*. Ithaca, N.Y.: Cornell University Press.

Peltzman, Sam. 1983. "Toward a More General Theory of Regulation." *Journal of Law and Economics* 19:211–240.

———. 1965. "Entry in Commercial Banking." *Journal of Law and Economics* 8:11–50.

Perkins, Dwight Heald. 1986. *China: Asia's Next Economic Giant?* Seattle: University of Washington Press.

The Planning Bureau, Council for Economic Research on the Pacific Region for the 21st Century. 1985. *Prospects for the Pacific Age: Economic Development and Policy Issues of the Pacific Region to the Year 2000*. Tokyo: Economic Planning Agency.

Pye, Lucian W. 1973. "The Concept of Political Development." In A. G. Kebschull (ed.), *Politics in Traditional Societies*. Appleton Century Crofts.

Raju, G. C. Thomas. 1983. *The Great Power Triangle and Asian Security*. Lexington, Mass.: Lexington Books.

Reinecke, Wolfgang. 1989. "Commercial Banks and the Internationalization of Finance: The Politics of Regulatory Reform and Global Cooperation." Manuscript. Yale University, Department of Political Science.

Repeta, Lawrence. 1984. "Declining Public Ownership of Japanese Industry." *Law in Japan* 17:153–184.

Republic of China, Executive Yuan. 1989. *Statistical Yearbook*.

Republic of Korea, Bureau of Social Welfare, Ministry of Health and Social Affairs. 1979. "Changing Family Patterns and Social Security Protection: The Case of Korea." In *International Social Security Association*, pp. 39–46. Report of the Regional Research Meeting on Changing Family Patterns and Social Security Protection. March. Canberra, Australia.

Rosenbluth, Frances McCall. 1989. *Financial Politics in Contemporary Japan*. Ithaca, N.Y.: Cornell University Press.

Salaff, Janet. 1988. "State and Family in Singapore: Restructuring an Industrial Society." Ithaca, N.Y.: Cornell University Press.

Schaede, Urike. 1988. "The Introduction of Commercial Paper: A Case Study in the Liberalization of the Japanese Financial Markets." Manuscript.

Schiffer, Johnathan. 1991. "State Policy and Economic Growth: A Note on the Hong Kong Model." *International Journal of Urban and Regional Research* 15, 2:180–196.

Scott, Ian. 1989. *Political Change and the Crisis of Legitimacy in Hong Kong*. Hong Kong: Oxford University Press.

Segal, G. 1983. *The Soviet Union in East Asia*. Boulder, Colo.: University of Colorado Press.

Semyonov, M., and N. Lewin-Epstein. 1989. "Segregation and Competition in Occupational Labor Markets." *Social Forces* 68, 2:379–396.

Shalom, Stephen. 1985. *The Sino-British Joint Declaration on the Future of Hong Kong*.

———. 1981. *The United States and the Philippines: A Study of Neocolonialism*.

Philadelphia: Institute for the Study of Human Issues.

Shukan Asahi. 1989. "Ninki no Supa MMC: Isoide Kau no wa Son Desu." Shukan Asahi (June 16):29–31.

Sit, Victor F. S., and Siu Lun Wong. 1989. Small and Medium Industries in an Export-Oriented Economy: The Case of Hong Kong. Centre of Asian Studies. Hong Kong: Hong Kong University Press.

Smart, James. 1989. The Political Economy of Street Hawkers in Hong Kong. Hong Kong: Hong Kong University Press.

Stigler, George. 1971. "The Theory of Regulation." Bell Journal of Economics and Management Science 12, 1:627–636.

Suh, S. M. 1987. "The Evolution of the Korean Economy: A Historical Perspective." Mimeograph. Korea Development Institute.

Suzuki, Yoshio. 1985. Kinyu Jiyuka to Kinyu Seisaku. Tokyo: Toyo Keizai Shimposha.

Syrquin, Moshe. 1988. "Patterns of Structural Change." In Hollis Chenery and T. N. Srinivasan (eds.), Handbook of Development Economics. Volume I. Amsterdam: Elsevier Science Publishers.

Tatsuzawa, Takuji. 1985. Watakushi no Ginko Showashi. Tokyo: Toyo Keizai Shimposha.

Teune, Henry, and Zdravko Mlinar. 1978. The Developmental Logic of Social Systems. Beverly Hills: Sage Publications.

Turner, H. A. 1980. The Last Colony: But Whose? Cambridge, Mass.: Cambridge University Press.

Un-Suh, Park. 1986. Korea's Economy. Washington, D.C.: Korea Economic Institute.

United Nations. 1988. Statistical Yearbook for Asia and the Pacific. Bangkok, Thailand: Economic and Social Commission for Asia and the Pacific.

U.S. Congress. 1973. Senate Committee on Foreign Relations Staff Report on Korea and the Philippines. Washington, D.C.: U.S. Government Printing Office.

Wallerstein, Immanuel M. 1976. The Modern World-System. New York: Academic Press.

West, Philip. 1987. Pacific Rim and the Western World. Boulder, Colo.: Westview Press.

Westphal, L. E., Y. W. Rhee, G. Pursell, et al. 1981. "Korea's Industrial Competence: Where It Came From." World Bank Staff Working Paper, No. 469. Washington, D.C.

Whitlam, Edward Gough. 1981. Pacific Community. Cambridge, Mass.: Harvard University Press.

Wong, A. W. F. 1980. "Non-Purposive Adaptation and Administrative Change in Hong Kong." In C. K. Leung et al. (eds.), Hong Kong: Dilemma of Growth, pp. 49–89. Canberra: School of Pacific Studies; and Hong Kong: Hong Kong University Press.

World Bank. 1988. World Tables, 1988–89 Edition. Baltimore: John Hopkins Press.

———. 1987. Philippines: A Framework for Economic Recovery. Washington, D.C.: World Bank.

———. 1986. World Development Report. New York: Oxford.

———. 1983. *World Development Report.* New York: Oxford.

Woronoff, Jon. 1986. *Asia's "Mirade" Economics.* Armonk, N.Y.: M.E. Sharpe.

Wyatt, David K. 1984. *Thailand, A Short History.* New Haven, Conn.: Yale University Press.

Young, John Dragon. 1985. "Socialism versus Capitalism: Towards a Hong Kong Strategy for Absorption Without Integration." In Y. C. Jao et al. (eds.), *Hong Kong and 1997: Strategies for the Future.* Centre of Asian Studies. Hong Kong: Hong Kong University Press.

Youngson, A. J. 1982. *Hong Kong: Economic Growth and Policy.* New York: Oxford.

Index

About the Editors and Contributors

RICHARD HARVEY BROWN is a Professor of Sociology at the University of Maryland, College Park, and President of the Washington Institute for Social Research. His current research interests are in the comparative political economy and cultural psychology of developing societies and advanced capitalist states. He has written or edited six volumes in this area. Dr. Brown is internationally reknowned as a theorist of the social sciences and has lectured in major universities of Europe, East Asia, Latin America, and the United States.

WILLIAM T. LIU is a founder of the Center for East-West Studies in Hong Kong. His research interests are in social change and East-West relations as they are associated with international migration. Dr. Liu's academic life includes more than a decade of teaching at the University of Notre Dame, where he served as Chairman of the Department of Sociology and Anthropology, Associate Dean of the College of Arts and Letters, Director of the Social Science Research and Training Institute, and Director of the Center for the Study of Man in Contemporary Society. He has written or edited 8 volumes, and more than 100 papers in scientific journals, chapters in books, and proceedings.

ELIEZER B. AYAL is on the faculty of the Department of Economics of the University of Illinois at Chicago.

GAVIN BOYD is Honorary Professor in the Department of Political Science of Rutgers University in Newark, New Jersey.

ALBERT CELOZA is on the faculty of the Department of Political Science of Phoenix College in Arizona.

B. KARIN CHAI is on the faculty of the Department of Sociology of Hong Kong Baptist College.

FREDERIC C. DEYO is on the faculty of the Department of Sociology of the State University of New York at Brockport.

MIGUEL E. KORZENIEWICZ is on the faculty of the Department of Sociology of Duke University in North Carolina.

ROBERTO P. KORZENIEWICZ is on the faculty of the Department of Sociology of the State University of New York in Binghamton.

TAEWON KWACK is on the faculty of the College of Commerce of Sopang University in Korea.

FRANCES McCALL ROSENBLUTH is on the faculty of the Graduate School of International Relations and Pacific Studies of the University of California in San Diego.